An Owner's Manual

12 Powerful

Principles and Practices for

Puzzled Parents

Marsha Snow

Printed in the United States of America

ISBN 978-1-949598-18-6

Cover photo and internal illustrations

licensed through Adobe Stock

Cover design ©2020 Pink Umbrella Books

www.MarshaSnow.com

CONTENTS

Introduction

To set the stage for this book, I need to tell you how I felt about parenting in the fall of 1980. I was a young mom in my late twenties with five children aged seven, six, four, fifteen months, and a newborn. The children had come rather quickly, and as we all know, **parents have never been trained to be parents.** Consequently, I had been using all the traditional, "by-the-book" parenting methods I could get my hands on. It seemed common sense to me that in order to be a good mother, I should apply a consequence or punishment when my child misbehaved to teach the child not to repeat that behavior.

How did it work? I had never felt so much frustration and failure in my life. My days were filled with my yelling, spanking, and denying privileges as I tried desperately to "control" my children's behavior. I realized after a time that these methods were not effective because they didn't seem to teach my children anything about handling the situation the next time it arose. Nevertheless, I didn't know what else to try. Parenthood was a puzzle that I just couldn't seem to solve.

I feel very fortunate that Heavenly Father answered my pleas for help at this time in the form of a friend named Deanne, who gently tutored me with patience and love, and pointed me in the direction that led to the path that I wanted to be on. Deanne was the mother of eight children, with her youngest child being the same age as my oldest child. She graciously held a little "mother class" in her home each week for a few of us floundering young moms where we could come and ask questions, share our frustrations, and feel encouraged and supported in our crucial roles as mothers. Most importantly, Deanne helped me to discover how to *really* love my children. For this I will be eternally grateful.

The pages that follow represent a compilation of over twenty years of my own personal study and research on parenting in my efforts to fulfill the sacred calling of being a mom. Over the years I have had opportunities to be a teacher and mentor to other parents who were seeking help. I have attempted to organize the principles I learned in a logical sequence and a workable format to help the pieces of the parenting puzzle fall into place.

So, what is the purpose of this book, and what sets it apart from the scores of books that have been written about parenting? Just as it was impossible for me to learn all I needed to know about parenting in one week from a class at Deanne's, it is impossible for anyone to do the same by simply reading a nice book about parenting. There are no quick fixes when it comes to parenting. This book is meant to be read and applied chapter by chapter as if the reader were taking a weekly class. Each chapter ends with an assignment, which should be practiced for one week before going on to the next chapter. As this procedure is patiently and carefully followed by one or both parents for each of the eight chapters in this book, I can promise that great things—even miracles—will occur in your family.

Let me share two of my favorite parenting quotes with you.

"The teaching, rearing, and training of children requires more intelligence, intuitive understanding, humility, strength, wisdom, spirituality, perseverance, and hard work than any other challenge we might have in life."[1]

James E. Faust

"We must work at our responsibility as parents as if everything in life counted on it, because in fact everything in life does count on it."[2]

Gordon B. Hinckley

Do you need some help with this daunting responsibility?
Chapter 1 will get you started.

Notes

1. James E. Faust, "The Greatest Challenge in the World—Good Parenting," *Ensign*, Nov. 1990, 32.
2. Gordon B. Hinckley, "Each a Better Person," *Ensign*, Nov. 2002, 100.

Chapter 1
Parenting Principles and Practices

Let's talk about family situations over the past few decades. In the past, it seemed easier to successfully raise a family because society was an ally, a resource. People were surrounded by role models, examples, media reinforcement, and family-friendly laws and support systems that sustained marriage and helped create strong families. Essentially, success in raising a family was more a matter of "going with the flow."

Life in the twenty-first century, however, isn't that simple anymore. Society doesn't support families as it used to. Life is more technological, faster, more sophisticated, scarier. Trends in wider society over the last thirty to fifty years have basically shifted from pro-family to anti-family, and to "go with the flow" today is family-fatal!

Since the challenge has changed, we must develop a response that is equal to the challenge. The desire to create a strong family is not enough. Even good ideas are not enough. We need a new mindset and new skills. We don't have to learn a hundred new practices or be constantly searching for newer, better techniques. All we need is a basic framework of fundamental principles that we can apply in any situation. Thus, the objective of this book:

We will learn correct principles and apply them in all family relationships.

Principles are natural laws that cannot be broken but, like lighthouses, will light our way. **Focusing on principles will have a far greater effect on behavior than focusing on behavior alone.**[1] We have all learned some principles thus far in our lives. This book teaches **correct** principles, universal principles that you already know in your heart to be true. You will have the opportunity as you read to decide if the principles you currently follow align with the correct principles presented here.

SOCIETAL ATTITUDES—OR PARADIGMS—ABOUT PARENTING

Before we go any further, it is important for you to do two things. The first is to understand your own *paradigm*—especially as it relates to parenting. Our paradigm is the way we view our situations, ourselves, our world. Think of a paradigm as a map of how you interpret the world. Our paradigms—correct or incorrect—are the sources of our attitudes, behaviors, and ultimately our relationships with others. Generally, we become emotionally and intellectually attached to our paradigms, and even when we are confronted with evidence that we may have an incorrect paradigm—we stubbornly stick with the wrong but familiar map.

The second is to be willing to experience the power of a paradigm *shift*. A paradigm shift is a distinctly new way of thinking about old problems—not that the former view was wrong—but that it restricted our vision. When you have a new paradigm—a paradigm shift—you will likely feel both exhilarated and humbled by it. **Exhilarated** because in making the shift you will not simply gain more knowledge, but you will gain a whole new way of knowing. **Humbled** because you will know improvements in the paradigm still will and must take place.

As you begin to understand your own parenting paradigm and are willing to make a paradigm shift if necessary, consider two important elements that have a great influence over the life of a child:

1) How parents view the nature of a child. Many perspectives about the nature of children have arisen over the years in our society that have shaped child-rearing practices for centuries. Understanding the nature of children is critical to the study of parent-child interactions.

2) How parents view their own role as parents. With a correct understanding of the true nature of children, parents will have a more correct view of the role they play in a child's development.

So, let's look at some of society's views of both the nature of children and the role a parent should play in the life of a child. The first three views have been around for centuries.

INNATELY EVIL. Some people have thought that children are innately evil because of the fall of Adam and Eve. Consequently, they believe children require harsh punishment to "beat the devil" out of them.

Parents who view their children as **innately evil** will look for and see the worst in them and will see their role as being morally superior to their children, entitling them to engage in any kind of parenting behavior—however damaging it may be to the child.[2]

INNATELY GOOD. Another view is that children are innately good—born innately pure, with an intuitive sense of right and wrong. Parents who view their children as **innately good** may feel little need to guide and discipline them and will see their role as accepting and embracing any behavior that arises naturally from the self—no matter what the behavior.[3]

BLANK SLATE. This view claims that children are much like a blank slate, neither evil nor good. Children are therefore, mostly shaped by their experiences.

Parents who view their child as a **blank slate** discount the agency of the child by suggesting that he or she is purely a product of the environment and will see their role as being wholly responsible for the fate of children by controlling and altering their environment.[4]

The final two societal views of a child's nature and parental roles gained prominence during the twentieth century.

BIOLOGICAL. This perspective suggests that biological characteristics play a role in children's dispositions and temperaments. Parents who believe that **biology** dictates behavior will see their role as insignificant because the child was born this way.

CONSTRUCTIVIST. This perspective, focuses on the individual's ability to interpret—or even to construct—his or her environment.

Parents who follow this theory believe that children have the ability to make their own choices and will apply their **own interpretation** to what they are taught. Consequently, they will see their role as insignificant in that children may naturally and unavoidably abandon or alter the values they are taught and "do their own thing."

THE CORRECT VIEW

Which of these societal views of children's nature and parents' roles is correct? Perhaps the best answer is none of them. Each contains some element of truth. However, without the knowledge that comes from God, each of these views—or a combination of them—falls short of the truth. Most important, none of these perspectives offers stable guidelines for moral behavior. These perspectives leave a sense of confusion about the true nature of children and about the exact responsibility a parent has toward a child.

So, where *do* we find the correct map? The restored gospel dispels confusion and offers us a correct parenting map in the form of "The Family: A Proclamation to the World." President M. Russell Ballard refers to this document as a clarion call to protect and strengthen families and further teaches, "The proclamation is a prophetic document, not only because it was issued by prophets but because it was ahead of its time."[5] Presented on September 23, 1995, the proclamation was indeed well ahead of the worldly attack on traditional families. Consider the headline of this newspaper article I clipped from the front page of our local newspaper in March 1998:

SERVING THE COMMUNITIES OF THE F

INC.   VOL. 50, NO. 61   **SATURDAY**

More single women are choosing to have children on their own

DITCHING DADDY

The future? Dr holds a sperm gen at the Pipo

BY SHERRY BOAS
THE TRIBUNE

A completely radical idea to me in 1998! This was the first time I remember seeing such a blatant attack on traditional families published in the daily newspaper, confirming the fact that the proclamation was certainly ahead of its time.

As worldly opinions continue to confuse us about children's nature and parents' roles, the proclamation teaches the correct nature of children and the vital role of parents:

> All human beings—male and female—are created in the image of God. Each is a beloved spirit son or daughter of heavenly parents, and, as such, each has a divine nature and destiny.
> "Children are an heritage of the Lord" (Psalm 127:3). Parents have a sacred duty to rear their children in love and righteousness, to provide for their physical and spiritual needs, and to teach them to love and serve one another, observe the commandments of God, and be law-abiding citizens wherever they live. Husbands and wives—mothers and fathers—will be held accountable before God for the discharge of these obligations.[6]

Without question, the proclamation clarifies these two important elements. Using the proclamation, scriptures, and words of prophets, we are not confused by society's views of children or about our duty as parents:

1) Because the **innately evil** view is rejected in the restored gospel, harsh discipline or severe physical punishment is not necessary.[7]
2) Although the restored gospel teaches that we are all **innately good**, children are not to be left to their own devices but are to be guided by parents and brought up in light and truth.[8]
3) In the **blank slate** view environment is everything; however, the restored gospel teaches that individuals have agency to choose their own destiny regardless of their environment.[9]
4) It is true that **biological** factors may affect children's dispositions and temperaments. There may even be some biological/genetic tendencies which make up part of the

"natural man" that must be overcome throughout life (Mosiah 3:19).

5) Children to some degree select, modify, and even **construct** their own environments according to their tendencies. Scientific evidence suggests that shared family influences are as important or even more important than genes in impacting the development of children. Therefore, the importance of rearing children in gospel-centered homes should not be underestimated.[10]

Parents must realize that variety in children may require a variety of responses from parents. In fact, Brigham Young encouraged parents to study their children's dispositions and temperaments and deal with them accordingly.[11] Put another way, in parenting, one size does not always fit all.

METAPHOR FOR A FAMILY

With our correct map in mind, we now need to realize that good families—even great families—are off track 90% of the time! The key is for great families to have a sense of destination, to know what the "track" looks like, and to keep coming back to it time and time again. It's like the flight of an airplane. Before the plane takes off, the pilots have a flight plan. They know exactly where they're going and start off according to their plan. But during the course of the flight, wind, rain, turbulence, air traffic, human error, and other factors act upon that plane. They move it slightly in different directions so that *most of the time* that plane is not even on the flight path! Nevertheless, barring anything too major, the plane will still arrive at its destination.

How does that happen? During the flight, the pilots receive constant feedback from instruments, from control towers, from other airplanes—even sometimes from the stars. Based on that feedback, they make adjustments so that time and time again, they keep returning to the flight plan.

The flight of an airplane is the ideal metaphor for family life. If the airplane represents daily life with regard to our families, it doesn't make any difference if we are off target or even if our family is a mess. The hope lies in the vision and in the plan and in the courage to keep coming back time and time again.[12]

THE VISION. Having a sense of destination—knowing what you want your family to be like—is critical. Each family has unique needs and unique situations. The list of struggles families face today is a long one: marriage, single-parenting, wayward children, rebellious teenagers, blended families, discipline, making ends meet, contentions—to name a few. You may be experiencing a combination of many of these or other stresses, leaving you with no sense of hope at all.

Whatever your situation, it is vitally important that you do not compare your family to any other family. No one will ever know the full reality of your situation, and you will never know the full reality of another family's situation. Our tendency is to think that other families are just about perfect while ours is falling apart. Every family has its challenges.

The wonderful thing about having a sense of destination is that you can envision what you want *your* family to be like—your family's unique destination. It doesn't have to look the same as anyone else's. The idea is to create a vision that is shared by everyone in the family.

THE FLIGHT PLAN. It is vital that we have a flight plan based on the principles that will enable us to arrive at our destination. What is our flight plan? It is the correct principles

11

that we are going to discuss in this book—principles based on the proclamation. Remember…**focusing on principles will have a far greater effect on behavior than focusing on behavior alone.**

Just as the pilot is off course most of the time, we will also have a difficult time staying right on the mark. But when our destination is clear and we know the plan, we can keep coming back to the flight plan time and time again. In fact, this journey is really part of the destination. How we travel is as important as where we arrive. Hope lies in the vision and in the plan and in the courage to keep coming back time and time again.

THREE PARENTING APPROACHES

Just as children have differing dispositions and temperaments, parents have differing ways of rearing their children. Some methods work better than others.

COERCIVE. Also known as the authoritarian approach, this is a hostile parenting style using frequent spanking, yelling, criticizing, and forcing children. Children are not invited to discuss rules or to express their feelings but are expected to accept parents' word for what is right. These parents value firm control, show little warmth, and are seen as the controllers of all aspects of children's development.

Outcomes of authoritarian parenting may result in immediate compliance in children, but children do not learn how to regulate their own behavior from within and tend to be anxious, have unhappy moods, and are hostile when they are frustrated. This approach shows little respect for the divine nature of a child and corresponds with the innately evil and blank-slate child views.

PERMISSIVE. The permissive parenting style either indulges children or neglects them. Parents tend to avoid using their authority at all costs and do not impose structure on children's time—such as bedtime, mealtime, or time spent watching TV and using electronic devices. Restrictions, demands for mature behavior, and consequences for misbehavior are kept at a minimum. These parents usually avoid confrontations and show warmth and love toward children, but they are shirking their divine duties by not taking responsibility for teaching their children the bounds of acceptable and unacceptable behavior.

Outcomes of permissive parenting result in children who have difficulty respecting others and coping with frustration. They tend to be impulsive, disobedient, and rebellious; have poor self-control and school performance; and have a higher rate of adolescent sexual activity and drug and alcohol abuse.[13] This approach is somewhat like the innately good view in that it is a child-centered perspective with an emphasis on the child's agency.

AUTHORITATIVE. Authoritative parenting fosters a positive emotional connection with children, provides for regulation that places fair and consistent limits on child behavior, and allows children reasonable latitude in decision-making. Parents have high expectations for their children and exert firm control, but do not hem in their children with restrictions. Instead, they encourage discussion and share the reasoning behind their policies. These parents show a high degree of warmth and responsiveness and are loving and supportive. At the same time, they are demanding in that they guide their children firmly and consistently require them to contribute to the family by helping at home. They willingly confront their children in order to obtain cooperation, state their values clearly, and expect their children to respect their norms.[14]

Outcomes of authoritative parenting result in children who are likely to be socially confident, friendly, self-disciplined, cooperative, high in self-esteem, and achievement-oriented. This approach is most consistent with the scriptures and teachings from Church leaders. This is proclamation-based parenting.

Proclamation-Based

Which are you?

Do you know which parenting style you use? Find out by determining which response you would give after reviewing the following situation:

You ask your nine-year-old son to eat his vegetables—broccoli tonight—and he just can't seem to stomach it. "I don't like broccoli," he complains.

1) "You'll eat that broccoli because I say so, even if you have to sit at the table all night."

2) "Okay, whatever…"

3) "I'm sorry you don't like it, but vegetables are an important part of a healthy diet. If you would prefer baby carrots, then go get a handful out of the refrigerator. But you will need to include some vegetables in your dinner tonight."

The three responses correspond respectively to the coercive, permissive, and authoritative approaches. Are you feeling any paradigms starting to shift? The important thing here is not that your son eat broccoli for dinner tonight but that he learns about healthy eating. He may or may not develop a taste for broccoli in the future, but he will learn more about responsible eating in the present as you correctly respond to him. The chapters of this book will teach you how to be an authoritative parent in *all* situations.

NINE PROCLAMATION PRINCIPLES

The proclamation gives nine principles for successful parenting: faith, prayer, repentance, forgiveness, respect, love, compassion, work, and wholesome recreational activities. These principles provide a foundation for parental influence that will help children return to live with Heavenly Father.

THE GREATEST OF THESE IS LOVE

All parents *love* their children. The challenge is to convey this love to the child. One of the greatest errors of today is the assumption that parents naturally convey the love they feel to their child. The truth is, many parents aren't transmitting love to their children. They just don't know how. Many children do not feel genuinely, unconditionally loved and accepted.

What is unconditional love? It is loving children *no matter what*. No matter what they look like; no matter what their assets or their liabilities; no matter what we expect of them; no matter *how they act*. It means that you love the child even though you detest the behavior. The most indispensable ingredients in your child's life are *you* and your *unconditional love* for them. This is the single most important thing you can do for your children.

> *We must ask daily for the gift of charity in order to truly be able to show unconditional love to our children*

Another word for unconditional love is charity. Charity is a gift from God. The scriptures teach us that we must ask for the gift of charity or unconditional love. The reason we must ask for this gift is that unconditional love requires more of us than we have to give without help from Heavenly Father.

President Thomas S. Monson wisely counseled:

> To you who are parents, I say, show love to your children. You know you love them, but make certain they know it as well. They are so precious. Let them know. Call upon our Heavenly Father for help as you care for their needs each day and as you deal with the challenges which inevitably come with parenthood. You need more than your own wisdom in rearing them.[15]

We must ask daily for the gift of charity in order to truly be able to show unconditional love to our children.

CONVEYING LOVE TO A CHILD. So how do we convey our

love to our children? Author Ross Campbell answers this question in his book *How to Really Love Your Child*.[16] He observes that children are continually asking their parents, "Do you love me?" They seldom ask this question verbally, but they ask it through their behavior. The answer to this question is the most important thing in the child's life and determines his basic attitudes. We answer through *our* behavior. Our love for a child is conveyed by what we **do** and **say**, but what we **do** carries more weight. A child is more affected by our actions than our words.

Dr. Campbell compares the emotional needs of a child to an emotional tank. Whether or not the tank is full (meaning his needs are met) determines how the child feels and behaves. The fuller the tank the more positive the feelings and the better the behavior. Only if his emotional tank is full can a child be expected to be or do his best. Only if his tank is full will he be happy, reach his potential, and respond to discipline.

Who keeps the tank full? The *parents*. Keeping children's emotional tanks full is the way that we convey our love to them. So how do we do it? How do we fill an emotional tank? There are three specific ways to do this: eye contact, physical contact, and focused attention. As we conclude this chapter, let's discuss the first way, eye contact, which is the first piece in our parenting puzzle.

EYE CONTACT. When we first think about eye contact, it may seem relatively unimportant to be included on a list of parenting skills. However, research findings conclude that eye contact is crucial in filling a child's emotional needs.[17] In fact, eye contact is one of the main sources of a child's emotional nurturing or filling the emotional tank. Of course, it is best received when accompanied by pleasant words and pleasant facial expressions, like smiling.

A word of caution: Unfortunately, without realizing it, we can use eye contact to send negative messages to our children. For instance, giving loving eye contact only under certain conditions, as when a child performs especially well, can come across as conditional love— which is exactly what we are trying to avoid.

Another terrible habit is using eye contact primarily when we want to make a strong point to a child, especially a negative one. When we use eye contact mainly for reprimanding and criticizing, this is a disastrous mistake. An even worse habit is actually avoiding eye contact as a punishment device. Consciously refusing to make eye contact with a child is usually more painful than physical punishment. It can be devastating and may be one of those incidents in a child's life that he will never forget. What we must understand is that we as parents must use eye contact as a continuous love-giving route and not merely as a means of discipline.

WEEKLY ASSIGNMENT

Your assignment for this week is to implement the first piece of the parenting puzzle by using positive eye contact with your children. Look at them when you speak to them and especially when they speak to you. Please don't make a big announcement about what you are doing. Just do it! Be aware of where your eyes are when you are with your children. You may be standing right next to a child, but your eyes may be focused elsewhere.

EYE CONTACT:

The first way to fill an emotional tank.

MOMENTS THAT MATTER MOST

"We would do well to slow down a little, focus on the significant, lift up our eyes, and truly see the things that matter most. Strength comes not from frantic activity but from being settled on a firm foundation of truth and light. It comes from paying attention to the divine things that matter most. Diligently doing the things that matter most will lead us to the Savior of the world." Dieter F. Uchtdorf [18]

GUIDING PRINCIPLES AND PRACTICES

Twelve parenting principles will be introduced throughout the eight chapters of this book. Each principle is connected to a **practice**—something one can actually **do** to apply the principle. At the conclusion of each chapter will be a summary of the principles and practices taught in that chapter.

Principle #1: Charity is essential.

Principle #2: A child's emotional tank must be filled.

Practice #1: Pray daily for the gift of charity.

Practice #2: Fill a child's emotional tank by expressing unconditional love to the child.

This Week

LOOK AT YOUR KIDS

Notes
1. Stephen R. Covey, *The 7 Habits of Highly Effective Families*, (New York: Golden Books, 1997), 15.
2. Craig Hart and others, "Proclamation-Based Principles of Parenting and Supportive Scholarship," *Strengthening Our Families*, ed. David C. Dollahite (Salt Lake City: Bookcraft, 2000), 101.
3. Ibid., 103.
4. Ibid., 102.
5. M. Russell Ballard, "What Matters Most Is What Lasts Longest," *Ensign*, Nov. 2005, 41.
6. "The Family: A Proclamation to the World," *Ensign*, Nov. 1995, 102.
7. "Proclamation-Based Principles," 102.
8. "The Family: A Proclamation," *Ensign*, Nov. 1995, 102.
9. "Proclamation-Based Principles," 102-3.
10. Ibid., 105.
11. *Discourses of Brigham Young*, sel. John Al Widtsoe (Salt Lake City: Deseret Book, 1954), 207.
12. Covey, *The 7 Habits of Highly Effective Families*, 9-10.
13. "Proclamation-Based Principles," 109.
14. Diana Baumrind, "Effects of Authoritative Parental Control on Child Behavior," *Child Development*, Dec. 1966, 353-54.
15. Thomas S. Monson, "Abundantly Blessed," *Ensign*, May, 2008, 112.
16. Ross Campbell, M.D., *How to Really Love Your Child*, (Wheaton: SP Publications, Inc., 1977).
17. Ibid., 45-47.
18. Dieter F. Uchtdorf, "Of Things That Matter Most," *Ensign*, Nov. 2010, 21.

Chapter 2
Building Quality Relationships:
The Marital Bond

Moments are the molecules that make up eternity! Years ago, President Gordon B. Hinckley advised, "It is not so much the major events as the small day-to-day decisions that map the course of our living."[1] As you continue to read, ponder, and apply the principles in this book you will be guided in your small daily decisions.

Proclamation-Based

EVALUATION OF EYE CONTACT ASSIGNMENT

Remember that eye contact is one of the main sources of emotional nurturing for children and should be used in positive ways. Never avoid eye contact with a child or use it only when you are displeased with him or her. Did you have some enlightening experiences looking at your kids this week?

Another important point to stress about eye contact is that it is never too early to give eye contact to a child. Infants begin to focus their eyes at two to four weeks of age, and the first image to hold an infant's attention is the human face—focusing on the eyes. At the age of two months an infant's eyes will lock on another set of eyes, feeding emotionally. Emotional tanks need filling at an early age.

What about teens? Young children may be receptive to eye contact continuously, but teens may have uneasy periods when they resist eye contact. Don't let this avoidance of eye contact irritate you. Try to accept it. The secret is to be *available*. If you remain available, teens will come to you when their emotional tank is dry.

In summary, eye contact is a simple but extremely powerful method of expressing unconditional love and filling the emotional tank. Your assignment will be to keep using eye contact but to also add the second method for filling the child's tank.

PHYSICAL CONTACT

Physical contact is one of the most obvious ways to show love to another person. However, when we consider physical contact, we are not referring to only hugging and kissing. A touch on the shoulder, a gentle poke in ribs, a tousle of the hair are each examples of appropriate physical contact to fill a child's emotional tank. Children need twelve touches a day[2]—touches that are natural and comfortable, not showy or overdone. When teens are not receptive to eye contact, physical contact can be used to compensate effectively. Simply touch the teen briefly on the shoulder, back, or arm as you walk by. They usually will not even notice it, but it registers in their mind.

Studies show that many parents touch their children only when necessary, such as when they are dressing and undressing them or carrying them to the car or to bed. Physical contact is an easy way to express unconditional love because you don't need a special occasion or an excuse to do it. Touch is one of love's strongest voices: It shouts, "I love you!" Research has shown that hugging increases oxytocin, a positive brain chemical, which not only lifts moods but reduces stress on the heart and improves the immune system. All children need to be touched. Wise parents will make every effort to provide many meaningful touches each day.

PHYSICAL CONTACT FOR BOYS. Boys' need for physical contact never ceases, but the needed type of contact changes with age. As infants, boys need to be held, cuddled, caressed, hugged, and kissed. This type of contact is *crucial* until they are seven or eight years old. Next comes "boy-style" physical contact (wrestling, giving "high fives", etc.). They never outgrow the need for **both** types. Boys, however, may tend to become unappealing and even irritating to us as they grow up, and we may not feel like physically expressing affection to a dirty, smelly little boy. When this happens, we must recognize and resist these unpleasant feelings and give him the physical contact he desperately needs. The younger the boy, the more important the physical contact. As a boy gets older, physical contact is harder to express because of the false assumption that a physical display of affection is feminine. The opposite is true: The more parents keep the emotional tank full—including using physical contact—the healthier the child's sexual identity will be.[3]

PHYSICAL CONTACT FOR GIRLS. The need for physical contact in girls increases in importance as she gets older—especially the more affectionate type of physical contact. This need reaches its peak at age eleven. Why is affectionate love so important to pre-adolescent-age girls? It prepares girls for adolescence. The two most important aspects of this preparation are to establish a girl's self-image and her sexual identity. As a young girl nears adolescence, it is vital for her to feel OK

about herself as a female. A father helps his daughter approve of herself by showing her that he approves of her. He does this by filling her emotional tank. The problem is that fathers usually begin to hold back physical contact just when daughters need it most.[4]

PHYSICAL CONTACT FOR TEENS. Although they may be bigger, stronger, and even smarter than their parents, teenagers are emotionally still children. They need to feel loved and accepted as never before. Don't stop hugging and kissing your teens. If they are not used to physical contact from you, don't overwhelm them with sudden large amounts. Obtain a baseline—a general idea of how much physical contact they can take—and gradually increase contact over the weeks. The less noticeable the increases the better.

PHYSICAL CONTACT:

The second way to fill an emotional tank. Remember to do it!

NURTURING A CHILD

Physical and eye contact combine to form the first essential piece of the parenting puzzle and are to be incorporated into all daily interactions with our children. They are two of the most effective ways to nurture a child or to fill a child's emotional tank. Nurturing your children—physically, emotionally, and spiritually—is one of the most important things you can do as a parent.

President Gordon B. Hinckley encouraged, "Take care of your little ones, welcome them into your homes and nurture and love them with all of your hearts."[5] Most parents desire to follow President Hinckley's advice. Unfortunately, busy mothers and fathers often feel puzzled about how to ensure that their children feel nurtured. A remarkable tool known as the Parenting Pyramid was created by Arbinger Institute and offers a remedy for this puzzling situation.

The layers of the pyramid represent various aspects of our lives. The solution to a problem in one level of the pyramid lies in the level just below it. For example, the apex of the pyramid is **correction**. If parents are having difficulty correcting their child (he ignores them or disobeys frequently) they must look to the level below correction—**teaching**. The effectiveness of our correction of our children, whatever method we use, will always depend on the effectiveness of our prior teaching.

So, the most important thing we can learn about correction is its dependence upon teaching. But no matter how much time I spend teaching my children, they are unlikely to learn much from me if they don't like me. Therefore, if I determine that my teaching is not effective, I look to the next level below and realize that I need to strengthen the **parent/child relationship**. Without a strong parent/child relationship, teaching can easily be construed as lecturing and be ignored. However, if this relationship is strong, the child will be more likely to respect and pay attention to the instruction given.

So, the effectiveness of our correction will depend upon the quality of our teaching, and the quality of our teaching will depend upon the quality of our relationship. If trouble is brewing in the parent/child relationship, we must look deeper into the pyramid to the central relationship in the home—the **husband/wife relationship**. In significant ways this relationship colors all others. Researchers have found that marital conflict is the most accurate predictor of childhood behavior problems.

Finally, the bottom layer of the pyramid directly affects every other part of the pyramid—our **personal way of being**. Fundamental to our success in all these layers is the personal example we set, our behaviors, attitudes, habits, and personal qualities.[6]

You will never be a better parent than you are a person.

To summarize: You will never be a better parent than you are a person.[7]

We will examine each layer of the pyramid beginning at the bottom.

PERSONAL WAY OF BEING

The parenting pyramid illustrates beautifully that the success of our relationships and parenting efforts rests upon who we *are* as people. As this is the deepest layer and foundation of the pyramid, how can we ensure that it is also the strongest layer? Let me share with you this secret:

THE MAGIC FIVE TO STAY ALIVE

1) Pray
2) Study
3) Exercise
4) Rest
5) Dress Attractively

These five things—which are not so secret—if done **every day** will create a personal way of being for you that will serve as a solid foundation for all the other layers of the pyramid. Let's quickly review these five "secrets."

PRAY. A kneeling prayer at least twice each day is the minimum here. For the remainder of the day, your heart should be drawn out in prayer continually, pleading for the Spirit to guide your every action.

STUDY. The scriptures and words of living prophets are the core of your study. An essential ingredient here is that you have a personal study plan that will work for you—your personality and schedule—and rigorously stick to it. Consistency is key!

EXERCISE. A companion to exercise is proper nutrition. Volumes have been written about exercise and nutrition. Keep exercise simple enough to make it a doable habit in your life. Eating nutritiously is a given. Make whatever sacrifices are necessary in your life to incorporate these secrets.

REST. The type of rest we are referring to here is the "early-to-bed, early-to- rise" type we are admonished to get in the scriptures (Doctrine and Covenants 88:24). Rather than stay up into the wee hours of the morning to finish a project, the better choice is to retire early and arise early to complete the project with an invigorated mind.

DRESS ATTRACTIVELY. At first glance, this secret may seem unusual to be included on a list of parenting skills. However, you will receive more respect from those in your home if you "get dressed" instead of lounging in pajamas for most of the day. The bottom line is, when you are dressed attractively your brain tells you that you are ready to accomplish something good—and you usually do!

HUSBAND/WIFE RELATIONSHIP

Which comes first? A good marriage or good parenting? While it may be possible to have a good marriage and not have good parenting skills, it is more difficult to be a good parent without a good marriage. Therefore, the most important relationship in the family is the marital relationship. The quality of the parent/child bond depends upon the quality of the marital bond. Strong families begin with strong marriages.

Of course, we know that some divorces are unavoidable. We all know good people—family or friends—who have experienced divorce. Dallin H. Oaks gives timely advice and words of encouragement to those in this category: "No matter how difficult your experiences, you have the promise that you will not be denied the blessings of eternal family relationships if you love the Lord, keep His commandments, and just do the best you can."[8] As we consider marital relationships in this book, we will not look to the past but only to today and to the future.

Are you satisfied with your marriage? The goal is to move from being satisfied with your marriage to being truly excited with your marriage. Whatever the quality of your marriage now, it can always be better. The greatest thing you can do for your children is to love your spouse. Harold B. Lee once noted, "A woman happy with her husband is better for her children than a hundred books on child welfare."[9] Children get much of their security from the way their parents treat each other. Therefore, building the marriage relationship will have a powerful effect on the family.

HOW CAN WE BUILD A MARRIAGE RELATIONSHIP?

We live today in a plastic world—a throw-away society—out with the old and in with the new as we look for shinier, newer, unblemished things. Marriage to the world has become another consumer game (if anyone marries at all). First marriages are often referred to as "starter" marriages. Latter-day Saint beliefs are in sharp contrast because we understand the eternal nature of the family. Bruce R. McConkie stated, "The most important single thing that any Latter-day Saint ever does in this world is to marry the right person, in the right place, by the right authority."[10] His further counsel emphasized keeping the covenants made. Worldly opposition to marriage comes from Satan, whose curse is to never be married and have children. For this reason, he is doing everything he can to attack marriage today because he wants us miserable like he is.

The place of marriage in the eternal scheme of things is so important that it deserves a lifetime of devotion. Success in marriage does not come automatically. Building a life together takes work, commitment and love. It has been said that marriage is the *end* of your troubles—but which end? There is no quick fix or magic formula for marriage success. Those who build a happy, secure, successful marriage pay the price to do so. They work at it *constantly*. We can't make everything right in marriage with a positive mental attitude. Natural laws and principles operate regardless of the circumstances.

PRESIDENT SPENCER W. KIMBALL'S MARRIAGE FORMULA

The closest thing to a magic formula for a successful marriage is given to us by a prophet. Spencer W. Kimball offers a four-step formula for success in marriage:[11]

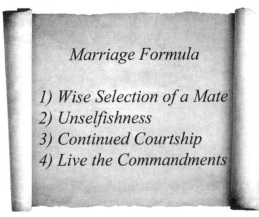

Marriage Formula

1) Wise Selection of a Mate
2) Unselfishness
3) Continued Courtship
4) Live the Commandments

Let's briefly explore each of these steps.

WISE SELECTION OF A MATE. The selection of a mate is a choice with eternal consequences. Dallin H. Oaks expresses beautiful counsel for the formula's first step:

> If you wish to marry well, inquire well. There should be dating, followed by careful and thoughtful and thorough courtship. There should be ample opportunities to experience the prospective spouse's behavior in a variety of circumstances. In all of this, we should realize that a good marriage does not require a perfect man or a perfect woman. It only requires a man and a woman committed to strive together toward perfection.[12]

For those of us who have already made the choice, does this mean we have to feel that we are "stuck with it"? Absolutely not! Remember that our emotions fluctuate. One day our mate looks perfect to us, and the next day we dislike them. When these fluctuations occur, it is wise to pause and recall all the reasons you chose your spouse in the first place. At one time he or she was the most appealing creature on earth to you. Although emotions will fluctuate, loyalty to our spouse does not.

We have access to a remarkable gift to assist us when our mate looks less than perfect. The Holy Ghost is this gift, and He can deepen our passions as we fast and pray for this blessing. Pray that you will feel about your spouse as you did on your wedding day. President Kimball shared this insight: "Don't just pray to marry the one you love. Pray to love the one you marry."[13] I like the suggestion that if you really want to know the nature of the person you married, read your spouse's patriarchal blessing. You will come to know you have married one of Heavenly Father's choicest spirits.

UNSELFISHNESS. One of the challenges we face today is to get rid of the worldly attitudes concerning relationships reflected in the following questions: "What's in it for ME?" "Are you meeting MY needs?" "Are you making ME happy?" Prophets have taught that divorce results from selfishness and pride. A solution to pride is humility. It takes humility to learn to say, "I'm sorry," even when you are not wrong. Richard G. Scott suggested:

> Marriage provides an ideal setting for overcoming any tendency to be selfish or self-centered. Don't withhold those natural expressions of love. Express gratitude for what your spouse does for you. Express that love and gratitude often. That will make life far richer and more pleasant and purposeful. Have faith in those promises and live to be worthy of them.[14]

Marriage is a profound commitment to **teach** each other. In a two-person relationship, we each must be as concerned about the other person's happiness as we are about our own. Make your first thoughts be, "What can I do to make my spouse happy?" Be positive in your interactions for the first five minutes of seeing each other after being apart for the day.

President Gordon B. Hinckley has observed, "A happy marriage is not so much a matter of romance as it is an anxious concern for the comfort and well-being of one's companion."[15] To overcome selfishness, we must do everything we can to seek the comfort and happiness of our mate.

CONTINUED COURTSHIP. Referring again to the proclamation's nine principles upon which successful marriages are established, love continues to be at the top of the list. But what do we mean by *love* in marriage? Hollywood's scripts would have us believe that love is a feeling. However, love—the feeling—is in reality a fruit of love—the verb. Since a verb is an action word, how do we *do* love?

I do not speak a foreign language, but my husband speaks German. If he expresses his undying love for me in German, his well-intentioned efforts will have been in vain. I will have no idea how he feels about me. Similarly, people speak different love languages. Your emotional language and that of your spouse may be as different as German and English. It is nearly impossible to *do* love with that type of language barrier.

There are basically five emotional love languages identified by Gary Chapman in his book *The Five Love Languages*.[16] Seldom do spouses speak the same language. The key to a loving marriage—

one in which we can *do* love—is to identify and learn to speak our spouses' love language.

Adults as well as children have emotional tanks (love tanks). Keeping a spouse's emotional tank full is as important to a marriage as keeping the proper amount of oil in a car. However, running a marriage on an empty love tank will cost much more than driving a car without oil. Who fills the love tank? The spouse. How do we fill the tank? Love tanks are filled by learning to effectively express—*do*—unconditional love to one another.

The "In Love" Experience. Most of us enter marriage this way. We meet someone we are attracted to, bells go off, and the game begins. This someone temporarily meets our emotional need for love and gives us a feeling that someone cares about, admires, and appreciates us. Our emotions soar because someone else sees us as number one, and they are willing to devote time and energy exclusively to our relationship. Our tank is full. We can conquer the world. Nothing is impossible. This is probably the first time in our lives that we have lived with a full tank. It is euphoric! We are both probably speaking all five love languages.

The problem with the "in love" experience is that it does not focus on our own growth nor the growth of the other person. Rather, it gives us the sense that we've already arrived. Our only desire is to stay there because this someone is perfect. The life span of this experience is two years or less. Hopefully, we marry during that time, but eventually we come down from our natural high and back to the real world. Our eyes are opened, and we see the warts of our spouse. Little traits we overlooked become huge mountains. The in-love experience was heavenly while it lasted. Our mistake was thinking that it would last forever.

We need to recognize the "in love" experience for what it was—a temporary emotional high. Now we must pursue "real love" with our spouse. Our most basic emotional need is not to **fall** in love but to **be** loved genuinely by someone, to know that someone **chooses** to love us. That kind of love requires effort and discipline. True love cannot begin until the "in love" experience has run its course. At that time, if our spouse speaks our love language, our need for love will be satisfied. If not, our tank will slowly drain, and we will no longer feel loved.

What are the Five Love Languages? A brief description of each language follows:

Mark Twain is credited for commenting, "I can live for two months on a good compliment." Six compliments a year would have kept his tank full. Your spouse will probably need more. Use words that build up: compliments, encouragement, words of kindness and appreciation. Possibly the deepest human need is to feel appreciated. Loving words of affirmation make requests and not demands. Requests create the possibility for an expression of love, while demands suffocate that possibility.

Each love language can also be used to negatively affect your spouse. For example, if your spouse's love language is words of affirmation, harsh or critical words spoken will be received as daggers.

Quality time means giving someone your undivided attention. It is not sitting on the couch watching television together but sitting on the couch with the television off—looking at each other and *talking.* Quality conversation is a vital component of quality time. Words of affirmation focus on what we are *saying,* whereas quality conversation focuses on what we're *hearing.* Learning to talk and listen to one another is a crucial part of this love language.

When quality time is your spouse's primary love language, checking your phone during a conversation together will be extremely hurtful. Another damaging practice is postponing previously arranged dates to spend time together.

The spirit of giving is at the heart of love, and all five love languages challenge us to give to our spouse. But for some whose primary love language is receiving gifts, gifts speak louder than words and are visual symbols of love. Some gifts are expensive; others are free. The cost doesn't matter. Almost anything you give will be received as an expression of love. Don't wait for special occasions to give your spouse a gift. This is one of the easiest love languages to learn.

An intangible gift that must not be overlooked is the gift of self or your physical presence in the time of crisis. This is the most powerful gift you can give if your spouse's primary love language is receiving gifts. Withholding your physical presence during a critical time is an example of a negative use of this love language.

Doing things you know your spouse would like you to do are acts of service. You seek to express your love by serving. Since the list of possible service opportunities is a long one, we must tell each other just what acts of service will fill our tank. Love is always freely given and cannot be demanded. We can request things of each other, but we must never demand anything. Requests give direction to love. Demands stop the flow of love.

A negative demonstration of this love language occurs when a spouse appears lazy to the one whose primary love language is acts of service. The laziness is manifested by not cleaning up after him or herself, making more work for the spouse who needs to be served to feel loved.

Physical touch can make or break a relationship. It can communicate hate or love. The touch of love may take many forms—running the hand through the hair, embracing, giving a back rub, holding hands, sexual expressions—all of these and other "love touches" are the emotional lifeline of the person for whom physical touch is the primary love language.

Appropriate physical touch sends a message far louder than words. Withholding touch or engaging in touch that is abusive in any way is devastating to a spouse whose primary love language is physical touch.

Discovering the Primary Love Language of Your Spouse. For you to keep your spouse's emotional tank full, it is essential that you know his or her love language. Part of this week's assignment and the second piece of the parenting puzzle is to discover one another's love language. Share with your spouse your primary love language. If you are not certain, think back to the "in love" experience. Ask yourself, "What did I like about my spouse? What did they say or do that drew me to them?" These memories will give you some idea of your primary love language.

The grass is always greener where you water it. Marriage is a living and growing thing which needs constant feeding. Weeds and tumors are also living things. Therefore, it is important to nurture with the correct love language. The day will come when the children leave home, and you will be left to enjoy your positive relationship or to suffer if you haven't worked to develop one.

Marriage is a covenant, and all covenants need renewing. Dating is more important after marriage than it was before. Babysitters are cheaper than marriage counselors. Create special ways and times that are right for you to have weekly time alone together. Recapture the feelings that led you to marry in the first place. Scheduling that time together will let your children know that your love for each other is important. Kids need a break from parents as much as parents do from kids. The sexual relationship is an ordinance between husbands and wives to renew the marriage vows and covenants and should be protected and cherished.

LIVE THE COMMANDMENTS. The last step in the formula is significant. A key to becoming closer as a couple is drawing closer to God and the Savior. If both are one with the Lord, the couple will have a celestial marriage. Just as a building needs a strong foundation, a family needs a strong foundation of Christ and His teachings. When we love God and Christ first, we will love our spouse more. Divine centeredness is the key to a celestial relationship.

Marriage Basics: Prayer, scripture study, temple attendance, service, charity (or unconditional love). Heavenly Father knows that we need help with our marriages. He wants us to have celestial marriages. Relationships are one of the only things we can take with us in our spiritual suitcases when we leave this life. When marriage is difficult, remember that whatever Christ lays his hands on is healed. As Christ performed physical healings, so He can heal relationships if we petition for help.

WEEKLY ASSIGNMENT

This week's assignment is two-fold: Use positive physical contact along with eye contact to keep the first puzzle piece in place, and discover the love language of your spouse to add the second important puzzle piece. To further assist you in discovering your love languages, you may enjoy reading Dr. Chapman's book or taking an online quiz to help determine your love language by visiting 5lovelanguages.com.

THINGS TO REALIZE

1) There are no perfect marriages.
2) We are all married to mortals.
3) No matter where you are in your marriage—it can always get better.

GUIDING PRINCIPLES AND PRACTICES

Principle #3: You will never be a better parent than you are a person.

Principle #4: The quality of the parent/child bond depends upon the quality of the marital bond.

Practice #3: Practice the "Magic Five to Stay Alive."

Practice #4: Nurture the marriage relationship.

This Week

PRACTICE POSITIVE TOUCH
WITH YOUR KIDS WHILE YOU
LOOK AT THEM

DISCOVER YOUR SPOUSE'S
LOVE LANGUAGE

Notes

1. Neal A. Maxwell, "The Tugs and Pulls of the World," *Ensign*, Nov. 2000, 37.

2. Virginia Satir, "Magic Touch: Six Things You Can Do to Connect in a Disconnected World" by Carolyn Rosenblatt, *www.forbes.com*, January 18, 2011.

3. Gary Chapman and Ross Campbell, *The Five Love Languages of Children*, (Chicago: Moody Press, 1997), 35.

4. Campbell, *How to Really Love Your Child*, 57-58.

5. Gordon B. Hinckley, "Excerpts from Recent Addresses of President Gordon B. Hinckley," *Ensign*, July 1997, 73.

6. The Arbinger Institute, "The Parenting Pyramid," *Strategies for Families*, 1998.

7. Joe J. Christensen, *One Step at a Time*, (Salt Lake City: Deseret Book, 1996), vii.

8. Dallin H. Oaks, "Divorce," *Ensign*, May 2007, 73.

9. Harold B. Lee, "Be Loyal to the Royal Within You," *https://speeches.byu.edu*, September 11, 1973.

10. Bruce R. McConkie, "Agency or Inspiration," *New Era*, Jan. 1975, 38.

11. Spencer W. Kimball, "Oneness in Marriage," *Ensign*, Mar. 1977, 4.

12. Oaks, "Divorce," 73.

13. *Marriage and Family Relations Participants Study Guide*, "Lesson 5," 18.

14. Richard G. Scott, "The Eternal Blessings of Marriage," *Ensign*, May 2011, 94.

15. Gordon B. Hinckley, "What God Hath Joined Together," *Ensign*, May 1991, 73.

16. Gary Chapman, *The Five Love Languages*, (Chicago: Northfield Publishing, 1992).

Chapter 3
Nurturing Parent/Child Relationships

Is there anything we ever do in this life that is harder than parenting? Yes. Marriage is not an easy venture, and marital happiness is a fragile thing that requires attention and effort to keep it healthy and alive.

EVALUATION OF LOVE LANGUAGE AND PHYSICAL CONTACT ASSIGNMENT

Do you know your love language and the love language of your spouse? Discovering and speaking your spouse's correct love language is a vital tool for nurturing the marital relationship and is an essential piece of our parenting puzzle. Understanding our moods is also extremely helpful. Between the high and low points on a continuum are an infinite number of mood levels. We constantly move up and down the mood continuum, changing our moods as often as the weather changes. Warmth, understanding, compassion, and a respectful sense of humor are the only forces that can help a person who is struggling with a low mood. With this understanding, we become grateful when our mood is high and graceful when it is low.[1] If we individually, and then jointly, seek the companionship of the Holy Ghost in our daily lives, our marriages will become stronger and happier. Whatever the quality of your marriage now—it can always be better.

The power of touch acts as a secret weapon by communicating positive emotions, providing a deeper sense of connection with others, and promoting feel-good sensations that foster a sense of well-being and happiness. Touch provides its own language of compassion. A pat on the back, a caress of the arm—everyday, incidental gestures that we usually take for granted—are far more profound than we usually realize. Is there an abundance of oxytocin flowing in your household currently? This "feel good" hormone is released every time we hug, so keep those hugs coming.

Remember: Good families—even great families—are off track 90% of the time! The key is for great families to have a sense of destination, to know what the "track" looks like, and to keep coming back to it time and time again.

Proclamation-Based

Each piece we add to the parenting puzzle more clearly defines the "track" leading to our destination. With the introduction of the first two pieces, giving positive eye and physical contact to children and speaking correct love languages to spouses, we are ready for the third puzzle piece.

FOCUSED ATTENTION

Eye contact and physical contact seldom require any real sacrifice. However, the third way to express unconditional love, focused attention, requires time—and sometimes a lot of it. Focused attention is giving a child your full, undivided attention in such a way that he feels without a doubt that he is completely loved and that he is the most important person in the world to his parents.

While viewing paintings of Christ with children, notice the high priority He gives to them. Such pictures show evidence of the three ways to fill an emotional tank: eye contact, physical contact, and focused attention. A child ought to be made to feel that he is the only one of his kind.

Focused attention is vital in a child's development of self-esteem and his ability to relate to other people, and it is the most demanding need of children. Yet, it is difficult for parents to recognize this need. Much of the misbehavior of children is an attempt for our time. To a child, negative attention is better than no attention. One reason parents may not recognize the need for focused attention is that other things they do seem to suffice, such as giving gifts and candy. Favors and gifts are easier to give because they take less time. These kindnesses are good, but they can't replace focused attention.

WHY IS IT SO DIFFICULT TO GIVE FOCUSED ATTENTION? Parenthood is expensive—it costs time. It is a 24-hour-a-day job for 365 days a year, except for leap year when we get to spend 366 days at it. We must face the facts: It is impossible to take care of every obligation and responsibility in our lives as we would like to. If we don't accept that, we will naively assume that everything will somehow be taken care of and become controlled by the tyranny of the urgent. Urgent matters will automatically control our lives and our time. Urgent matters (such as the phone) aren't always important matters. There is not enough time in our lives to be controlled by the urgent.

A popular saying suggests that children spell "love" T-I-M-E. We can tell them we love them—and we should—but spending time with them through focused attention will demonstrate that love isn't just something you *say*, it's something you *do*. If we don't spend time with people, we won't know them. The best way to give focused attention is to set aside time to spend alone with each child—to put them into your schedule. Simply ask the child to list some things he or she would like to do with you and schedule your time accordingly. Ideally, each child should have some individual time every day with each parent. This can be difficult in large families. We each must find our own way to do this. Watch for unexpected moments when you are alone with a child, whether it is five minutes or fifteen minutes. Tuck-ins at bedtime are ideal times for one-on-one focused attention. We must pay the price! We schedule other people into our calendars. Why not our children? Though it may be short—every moment counts.

Time spent with our children is like making deposits into a savings account—an investment in the future. Every deposit of time with a child is an assurance that the child's teenage years will be healthy, wholesome, pleasant and rewarding for the child and for the parent. What's more wonderful than a well-balanced teenager? What's worse than a wayward adolescent son or daughter?

WHAT ABOUT SINGLE PARENTS? Single parents have a particularly difficult time because there's no one there to help them out. They are doing all of it by themselves. In most cases, single parents report their greatest successes with focused attention when they enlist their children in helping with the jobs that need to be done in the family. Together they do the dishes, clean the house, cook the meals—and talk as they do these activities.

Special blessings come to parents who are doing it on their own. Single parents will never be able to do everything they want to with their children, but they will learn that the most important things can be accomplished. President Gordon B. Hinckley encouraged single parents to "do the very best you can." He went on to affirm the importance of making parenting a priority:

> As the years pass, you will become increasingly grateful for that which you did in molding the lives of your children in the direction of righteousness and goodness, integrity and faith. That is most likely to happen if you can spend adequate time with them.[2]

THE KEY IS TO DETERMINE OUR PRIORITIES. Where do our children fit in? *We must* control our time in order to take care of the important things. Priorities seem to fall quickly into place when one is faced with a terminal illness. A person's outlook on life is transformed, and a paradigm shift occurs with the realization that there is not enough time for everything. Less important things are resisted.

The story of Rick. A father was sitting in his living room one day. It was his fiftieth birthday, and he happened to be in an irritable mood. Suddenly, eleven-year-old Rick bounced into the room, sat on his father's lap, and began kissing him repeatedly on the cheeks. The boy continued his kissing until his father sharply asked, "What are you doing?" Rick answered, "I'm giving you 50 kisses on your fiftieth birthday." Ordinarily the father would have been touched by this loving act of affection. Unfortunately, because he was depressed and irritable, he pushed Rick away and stated, "Let's do that some other time." Crushed and embarrassed, Rick ran out of the house, jumped on his bike, and rode away. A few moments later he was struck and killed by a car. You can imagine the grief, remorse, and guilt suffered by this poor father.[3]

A perfect day. Let's look at another story illustrating the importance of focused attention. In the diary of the father of a great humanitarian was found a description of a day spent fishing with his son. The father laments how the day was a "total loss" because the son seemed "bored and preoccupied, saying very little." The father even wrote that he probably would not take his son fishing again. Many years later a historian found these notes, and with curiosity compared them with the entries of the same day in the son's diary. The son exclaimed what a "perfect day" it had been, "all alone" with his father. He described how deeply meaningful and important it was to him.[4]

These examples illustrate several things. First, because life is so unpredictable, we cannot know how many opportunities we'll have to nurture our children—to give them focused attention. Secondly, these moments don't happen every day. We must take advantage of timely opportunities because they are fewer than we may realize. Our children are growing up! Special moments leave lasting impressions on a child—either positively or negatively. If Rick's father had been able to spend those few moments with Rick in a positive way, Rick would have affectionately remembered that time the rest of his life. However, if Rick had not been killed, he would never have forgotten the pain, anguish, and humiliation of that moment.

Most powerful way of keeping an emotional tank full. Focused attention is time-consuming, difficult to do consistently, and sometimes burdensome to already exhausted parents. However, this piece of the parenting puzzle is the most powerful means of keeping a child's emotional tank full and investing in his future.

FOCUSED ATTENTION: Plan your time in order to give focused attention to each child.

SUMMARY OF WHAT THE PARENTING PYRAMID TELLS US

As we look at the parenting pyramid we can see that although correction is a part of parenthood, *it is the smallest part.* We've learned that the solution to a problem in one level of the pyramid lies in the level just below it. Therefore, the key to effective correction is effective teaching. The key to effective teaching is a good parent/child relationship. The key to a good parent/child relationship is a good husband/wife relationship. The key to a good husband/wife relationship is our personal way of being. This quality affects every other aspect of the pyramid—that is why it is the deepest foundation. If we try to correct our children when the other elements of the pyramid are not in place, *our correction will always be wrong.*

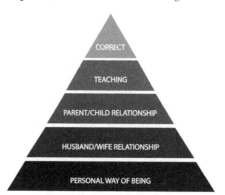

PARENT/CHILD RELATIONSHIP

Let's discuss relationships. It is amazing that some members of the Church of Jesus Christ of Latter-day Saints would not dream of sipping iced tea or fudging on tithing, yet they feel justified in ignoring principles for successful relationships. Relationships are one of the only things we take with us.

The most important relationship in the family is the marital relationship. The quality of the parent/child bond depends upon the quality of the marital bond. The stronger and healthier this bond is, the fewer the problems we encounter as parents. The only couples whose relationships don't suffer during child-bearing years are those who plan and protect their time and activities together.

UNCONDITIONAL LOVE IS THE FOUNDATION

Once the marital bond is in place, the foundation of a solid relationship with the child is unconditional love. Without this foundation, parenting is a confusing, frustrating burden. We effectively express unconditional love by using positive eye contact, positive physical contact, and appropriate focused attention with our children.

PRAY FOR THE GIFT OF CHARITY

We must constantly pray for the gift of charity or unconditional love as taught by President M. Russell Ballard:

> Brothers and sisters, may I re-emphasize that the most important attribute of Heavenly Father and of His Beloved Son that we should desire and seek to possess within our lives is the gift of charity, 'the pure love of Christ' (Moroni 7:47). From this gift springs our capacity to love and to serve others as the Savior did. The prophet Mormon taught us the supreme importance of this gift and told us how we can receive it: "Wherefore, my beloved brethren, pray unto the Father with all the energy of heart, that ye may be filled with this love" (Moroni 7:48).[5]

> *All behavioral problems are relationship problems.*

It is much easier to feel love for someone when you feel the Father's love for them. The more genuine and unconditional the love-bond from parents to children, the more positive is the relationship. All behavioral problems are relationship problems.

You cannot positively influence your children (or anyone) until you have a relationship with them. As Plato stated this important principle, "Whom can I teach but my friends?" We must have a relationship with a child before anything else—before teaching, before guidance, before example, *before* discipline.

BUILD A "COME UNTO ME" RELATIONSHIP

Think about the relationship we have with Heavenly Father and the Savior. When we make mistakes the Savior doesn't say, "Go to your room." He says, "Come unto me." This can be the example for the relationship we have with our children.[6] With a foundation of unconditional love in place, there are three ways to strengthen relationships with children or to build a "Come Unto Me" relationship with them:

- ♥ Understand child development
- ♥ Listen to understand
- ♥ Be kind

UNDERSTAND CHILD DEVELOPMENT. When we understand that children grow and develop in stages, we will treat a child in appropriate ways for his age. For example, infants will cry. Therefore, we will do our best to fill their basic needs without being upset with their crying. Toddlers will get into things. We will attempt to childproof their environment without being displeased with them. Two and three-year-olds are learning to be independent—they wiggle and have an attention span of about five minutes. As a result, we won't expect them to sit still for very long. In fact, even a four-year-old cannot sit still through an entire church service. Four and five-year-olds are in a mischievous stage and need to use their muscles. Don't be surprised when they use their muscles to push someone. Speaking

44

of muscles, did you know that running rather than walking is a child's normal means of locomotion? Other developmental considerations we must make: Accept that a clean shirt on a normal child will not stay clean for long; remember that trees are for climbing, mirrors are for making faces, and ten-year-old girls cry!

Accept the childishness of children. While we need to help children learn to control behavior that is not constructive, it is helpful to remember that some actions are not necessarily misbehavior but that the child is being the best he can be for his age. We must constantly remind ourselves that they are children. They will tend to act like children, and much of childish behavior is unpleasant. If we do our parts as parents and love them despite their childish behavior, they will be able to mature and give up childish ways.

Christ is the perfect example of this principle. He was patient with imperfections and maintained a loving relationship despite imperfect behavior. He showed respect for the person but didn't condone the misbehavior or ignore it. When attitudes needed correcting, He taught them—leaving no room for misunderstanding.

Too often we view our children more as objects than as individuals. We treat them as we would a vacuum cleaner—pushing them around or putting them away when not in use. When we forget that our children deserve our respect, our relationship with them becomes one of corrections and commands: "Make your bed." "Do your homework." "Go to your room!" When we remember that our children are fascinating, growing individuals, we soon desire to spend time with them. We enjoy learning about their interests, and their interests expand our own. As our relationship becomes one of mutual respect, we spend more time being with them. We need less time to correct negative behavior.

Appreciate personality differences. Brigham Young's counsel for parents to study their children's dispositions and temperaments strongly applies here. The more you understand your children's *natures*, the more you can *nurture* all the qualities they have to their advantage. The temperaments of introversion and extroversion are on opposite ends of an energy continuum. Where we fall on that continuum predicts how we derive our life energy. People on the more introverted end of the continuum focus inward to gain energy while those on the more extroverted end of the continuum focus outward to gain energy. In other words, introverts need alone time for recharging their batteries, which have been drained just by being around people and activity. On the other hand, extroverts are energized by activities, people, places, and things and need to be out and about to recharge their batteries.

Many children feel pressured, by parents or peers, to be extroverted because of our culture—75% of the world is extroverted![7] Since they are outnumbered three-to-one, introverted children need careful nurturing by understanding parents. Being introverted is not the same as being shy. Shyness is a state of anxiety wherein a person is afraid of rejection, ridicule, or embarrassment. Introversion is about how a person recharges his or her energy.

How do you determine what disposition your child has? Few children are extreme one way or another, and sometimes introverts act extroverted and vice versa. But the fact to remember is that the temperaments of introversion and extroversion are hard-wired into the brain. One is not better than another. Both deserve to be understood and embraced by parents. The following lists may be helpful as you consider your children's dispositions and temperaments.

Children who are primarily introverts will probably:
- Watch and listen before joining an activity.
- Concentrate deeply on subjects of interest.
- Enjoy time alone in their room.
- Speak after thinking things through.
- Have a strong sense of personal space and dislike people sitting too close or coming into their room without knocking.
- Be private and may need to be asked what they are thinking or feeling.
- Need validation; may have irrational self-doubts.
- Talk a lot if the topic is interesting or if they are comfortable with the people.

Children who are primarily extroverts will probably:
- Be gregarious and outgoing, except during normal developmental stages.
- Be energized by interactions and activities.

- Want to tell you all about their experiences and ideas immediately, covering lots of topics.
- Think out loud. They'll walk around the house saying, "Where's my ball?" as they hunt for it. They need to talk in order to make decisions.
- Prefer time with others rather than time alone.
- Need lots of approval. For example, they need to hear what a good job they are doing or how much you like their gift.
- Like variety and be easily distracted.
- Often volunteer what they are thinking or feeling.[8]

Remember, it's not about social skills; it's about how your child recharges his or her energy. The better you understand your children's temperaments, the more you can help them be able to use their temperament for fulfilling and valuable lives.

Respond appropriately to behavior. Children often engage in behavior that parents may not like, such as thumb-sucking, climbing, exaggerating, etc. Sometimes these unwanted behaviors are associated with developmental stages and are abandoned as children mature. Knowing that children grow and develop through stages, parents will feel less guilty and worried when these acts occur and will be able to respond to them more effectively.

Parents sometimes unknowingly reinforce unwanted behavior by punishing, ridiculing, or berating the child. This draws undue attention to the behavior, sometimes provoking the child to feel bad, defiant, or curious about the behavior. For example, if parents display an extreme response to thumb-sucking, this may provoke the child to cling to the behavior. If parents respond in an easygoing way or ignore it altogether, the child may be more likely to abandon it when it no longer serves a purpose.

Too much emphasis on age-appropriate behavior may reinforce it unnecessarily, encouraging the child to repeat the behavior excessively—even in ways that are unsafe. For example, if parents make a fuss over a toddler's climbing by saying, "He's so adorable when he does that," this may encourage behavior that could endanger the child's safety.

Teenagers often withdraw from family involvement and are critical of their parents. Parents who take this personally will feel rejected and try to impose control over their teen, which may provoke the child to rebel and hinder his progress through this phase of development. If parents take this behavior in stride without becoming overly concerned, this will enable the child to move through this phase. Generally, children become more accepting of their parents as they approach adulthood.

LISTEN TO UNDERSTAND. In striving for a "Come Unto Me" relationship, listen to children in such a way that they are sure you understand how they feel. Sometimes we are so busy regulating our children that we don't take time to listen to them. Children are more likely to listen to us and respond positively to discipline when they know they are listened to and understood. "Seek first to understand; then to be understood."[9] Listen with your heart for the unspoken message. When a child says, "I hate you!" he probably means, "I don't like the way I feel. I'm frustrated, and I don't know how to fix it."

When a Primary teacher says your child is a problem in class, instead of saying, "Were you noisy today?" listen first to what the child says about the experience. Not "Go to your room!" but "Come unto me." "Tell me about Primary. What is your favorite part? What happened in class today? If you could change Primary in any way, how would you change it?" By really listening to a child, you learn more about him and why he acts the way he does. You can respond in ways to help him. Many times, it is only their lack of experience that causes children to make mistakes.

Listening to understand is a valuable communication skill that will strengthen family relationships. Parents can help their children feel valued and respected by listening to them and accepting their feelings. Sometimes children have feelings that parents may not like. However, undesirable feelings often change when children are allowed to talk about them. For example, a child's feeling of anger toward a parent will often quickly turn to love when the child is allowed to talk about his feelings without being condemned. Children become frustrated and confused when their feelings are discounted or denied. They may even learn to distrust what they feel. Young children depend on their parents to help them make sense of their emotions. President Russell M. Nelson shared these thoughts:

The time to listen is when someone needs to be heard. Children are naturally eager to share their experiences, which range from triumphs of delight to trials of distress. Are we as eager to listen? If they try to express their anguish, is it possible for us to listen openly to a shocking experience without going into a state of shock ourselves? Can we listen without interrupting and without making snap judgments that slam shut the door of dialogue? It can remain open with the soothing reassurance that we believe in them and understand their feelings.[10]

As you give focused attention to each child:

LISTEN TO UNDERSTAND

BE KIND. As you strive to build relationships with your children, remember to be kind to them. Kindness to a child can be expressed in many ways. We don't have to add kindness to a list to do later. It can be as simple as a kind look or a gentle touch. Your tone of voice can be kind as you look into a child's eyes and speak to him. A valuable suggestion is to use *requests* vs. *commands* when speaking with a child. "Will you please bring that book to me?" instead of "Bring me that book." To *tell* is to preach—to *ask* is to teach. We should always *teach*, not *tell*, correct principles. The importance of kindness to a child cannot be overstated. "It's nice to be important, but it's more important to be nice."[11]

Keep in mind that it is impossible not to communicate. President Spencer W. Kimball once said, "Our expressions, our voice tones, our movements, our thoughts betray us."[12] Again—all communication should reflect kindness.

Let's consider some common communication practices, which may not be too kind, that drive children away from us. As you read these inappropriate examples of communication, make note of the ones you may have used or the ones you currently use and need to change.

- Lecturing, moralizing, preaching, interrogating.
  "If I've told you once, I've told you a thousand times. Can't you get it through your thick head that . . ."
  "You should be ashamed of yourself. Now look at what you've done."
  "Why in the world did you do that?"
- Discounting, placating, providing empty reassurances.
  "Calm down. There's no reason to be upset."
  "Okay, whatever it takes to make you happy."
  "Everything will be okay. Lots of people have suffered worse."
- Judging, condemning, threatening.
  "The trouble with you is . . ."
  "You'll never amount to anything."
  "Try that again and you won't sit down for a week."
- Blaming, criticizing, ridiculing.
  "It's all your fault."
  "You're so irritating."
  "I can't stand it when you whine like that."
- Talking about one's own feelings when a child needs to share his or her feelings.
  "I know exactly how you feel. When I was your age, I . . ."

The first step in improving communication is to recognize when a change needs to be made and be persistent in making the change.

The willingness of children to listen and talk often depends on the climate for communication parents create in the home. The Savior provides the supreme example of how we ought to be and how we ought to communicate with each other. The scriptures indicate that Jesus was slow to condemn, forgiving, compassionate, considerate of His family, willing to return good for evil, loving of children, appreciative, eager to serve, and willing to sacrifice. Parents who communicate in a Christlike manner can more easily stay on the track of proclamation-based parenting.

TIMELY COUNSEL FOR PARENTS

Elder Robert D. Hales offers this encouragement to parents:

> To truly understand the hearts of our youth, we must do more than just be in the same room or attend the same family and church activities. We must plan and take advantage of teaching moments that make a deep and lasting impression upon their minds and hearts. For our interactions to truly touch their hearts, we have to pay attention to them, just as we pay attention to a trusted adult colleague or a close friend. Most important is letting them talk, then asking them questions. And then being willing to listen—yes, listen and listen some more.[13]

WEEKLY ASSIGNMENT

This week as you continue to look at and to positively touch your kids, you will add the third piece of the puzzle and give focused attention to each child as you listen to understand their hearts. In addition, now that you know the love language of your spouse, your assignment will be to speak the love language of your spouse at least three times to keep the second piece in place.

GUIDING PRINCIPLES AND PRACTICES

This Week

GIVE FOCUSED ATTENTION TO EACH CHILD AS YOU LISTEN TO UNDERSTAND

SPEAK SPOUSE'S LOVE LANGUAGE THREE TIMES

Principle #5: All behavioral problems are relationship problems.
Practice #5: Build a "Come Unto Me" relationship.

51

Notes
1. George S. Pransky, *The Relationship Handbook*, (LaConner: Pransky and Associates, 2001), 43.
2. Gordon B. Hinckley, "Women of the Church," *Ensign*, Nov. 1996, 69.
3. Campbell, *How to Really Love Your Child*, 66.
4. Ibid., 67.
5. M. Russell Ballard, "Finding Joy through Loving Service," *Ensign*. May 2011, 49.
6. Michaelene P. Grassli, "Teaching Our Children," *Ensign*, April 1994, 62.
7. Marti Olsen Laney, *The Introvert Advantage*, (New York: Workman Publishing, 2002), 15.
8. Ibid., 131.
9. Covey, *The 7 Habits of Highly Effective Families*, 201.
10. Russell M. Nelson, "Listen to Learn," *Ensign*, May 1991, 22.
11. Mormonad, *New Era*, Jan. 2011, 15.
12. In Conference Report, Apr. 1954, 106.
13. Robert D. Hales, "Our Duty to God: The Mission of Parents and Leaders to the Rising Generation," *Ensign*, May 2010, 95-96.

Chapter 4
Listening to and Naming Feelings

By now you should be familiar with the keys to staying "on track' as parents: 1) Have a sense of destination. 2) Know what the "track" looks like. 3) Keep coming back to it again and again.

Proclamation-Based

EVALUATION OF LOVE LANGUAGE, FOCUSED ATTENTION, AND LISTENING ASSIGNMENT

Are you getting better at speaking your spouse's love language? Practice makes perfect! Continue the practice of looking for ways to communicate love in the correct language of your spouse to build and strengthen your marriage. Remember—whatever the quality of your marriage now, it can always be better.

Are you finding specific ways to spend time with each child? The key to focused attention with children is that it must be intentional and deliberate. Sometimes being busy is what we brag about, and unless we make plans to spend time together in a connecting way, it probably will not happen.

Listening to understand is one of the essential elements for building a "Come Unto Me" relationship. As you give focused attention, are you listening in such a way that your child is sure you understand how he feels? Continue seeking first to understand and then to be understood.

"COME UNTO ME" RELATIONSHIP REVIEW

Our foundation of unconditional love for our children will be continuously strengthened as we daily give eye contact, physical contact, and focused attention to each child. This foundation makes it possible for us to build a "Come Unto Me" relationship with them. Three essential elements for building this relationship are the following:

♥ Understand child development
♥ Listen to understand
♥ Be kind

There is, however, a fourth element that is absolutely vital for parents to possess.

EMPATHY, THE FOURTH ELEMENT

Let's discuss emotions. Much of today's popular advice to parents ignores the world of emotion. Instead, it relies on child-rearing theories that address children's misbehavior, but disregard the feelings that underlie that misbehavior.[1] It is important for a child to understand that it is normal to *feel*. Feeling is the very process of living. There are many ways to die other than physical death. We can die emotionally. We can stop feeling.

At times children are angry or sad. They cry, and they have fears. We often aren't very patient with those feelings. We have inherited a tradition of discounting children's feelings simply because children are smaller, less rational, less experienced, and less powerful than the adults around them. Taking children's emotions seriously requires the powerful qualities of empathy, keen listening skills, a willingness to see things from their perspective, and a certain selflessness. Did you know that preschoolers typically have some kind of need or desire to be dealt with at an average rate of *three times a minute?*[2]

- ♥ Understand child development
- ♥ Listen to understand
- ♥ Be kind
- ♥ Show empathy

Without these powerful qualities, life with a preschooler will be frustrating.

HOW IS IT THAT EMPATHY CAN BE SO POWERFUL? It is because empathy allows children to see their parents as allies.[3]

The story of William. Eight-year-old William looked very dejected as he came in from the yard because the kids next door refused to play with him. His dad looked up from his newspaper just long enough to say, "Not again! Look, William, you're a big kid now, not a baby. Don't get upset every time somebody ignores you. Just forget about it. Call one of your buddies from school. Read a book. Watch a little TV."

Because children usually believe their

> *Empathy allows children to see their parents as allies.*

parents' assessments, chances are William is thinking, "Dad's right. I'm acting like a baby. That's why the guys next door don't want to play with me. I wonder what's wrong with me. Why can't I just forget it like Dad says? I'm such a wimp. Nobody wants to be my friend."

Now let's replay the same situation with William's father responding differently when William comes in. What if Dad puts down his newspaper, looks at his son, and says, "You look kind of sad, William. Tell me what's going on."

If Dad listens—*really* listens with an open heart—perhaps William will come up with a different assessment of himself. The conversation might continue like this:

> William: Tom and Patrick won't let me play basketball with them.
> Dad: I'll bet that hurt your feelings.
> William: Yeah, it did. It made me mad, too.
> Dad: I can see that.
> William: There's no reason why I can't shoot baskets with them.
> Dad: Did you talk to them about it?
> William: Nah, I don't want to.
> Dad: What do you want to do?
> William: I don't know. Maybe I'll just blow it off.
> Dad: You think that's a better idea?
> William: Yeah, 'cuz they'll probably change their minds tomorrow.

I think I'll call one of my friends from school, or read a book. Maybe I'll watch some TV."

The difference, of course, is empathy. In both scenarios, Dad is concerned about his son's feelings. Perhaps he's been worried for a long time that William is "oversensitive" to his playmates' rejections; he wants his son to get tougher. In the first scenario, however, Dad made the common mistake of letting his own goals for William get in the way. Instead of empathizing, he criticized, gave a mini-lecture, and offered unsolicited advice. As a result, his well-intended efforts backfired. William walked away feeling more hurt, further misunderstood, and more like a wimp than ever.

By contrast, Dad in the second scenario took time to listen to his son and made it clear that he understood William's experience. This helped William feel more comfortable and surer of himself. In the end, William came up with the same solutions his father might have offered, but this time he owned the solutions and walked away tougher and with his self-respect intact.[4]

That is how empathy works. When we seek to understand our children's experiences, they feel supported. They know we're on their side. When we refrain from criticizing them, discounting their feelings, or trying to distract them from their goals—they let us into their world. They tell us how they feel. They offer their opinions. Our children begin to trust us.

Empathy is simply the ability to put yourself in your child's shoes and respond accordingly. Just because empathy is a simple concept, however, doesn't mean it is always easy to practice.[5]

WHAT HAPPENS WHEN A CHILD'S FEELINGS ARE DISMISSED? Many well-meaning parents dismiss children's negative feelings as though they didn't matter—laughing in the face of a raging preschooler, or telling a five-year-old who wakes up crying from a nightmare that "There's nothing to be afraid of" (when we have no idea what they just saw in their dream).

What happens to the child in such situations is that he begins to accept the adult's estimation of the event and learns to doubt his own judgment. With adults constantly invalidating their feelings, children lose confidence in themselves. Parents get impatient, angry, or try to correct by using trite phrases such as the following: "Oh, there's no reason to feel sad. Buck up and go on. Shake it off." "You shouldn't be jealous. That's not nice." "Don't be silly. There's nothing to be afraid of."

Over time, children assume that if so many feelings that come from inside and are part of them are wrong, then they themselves must be wrong inside—they themselves must be bad. Or they learn to distrust or reject their feelings. Afterall, most feelings seem to be wrong. You're not supposed to have them. If you do have them—it is not wise to share them.

EMOTION COACHING

Psychologist John Gottman of the University of Washington conducted a 20-year study of 119 families and found that couples who had the greatest parenting success were able to help their children when their children needed help the most—when they were distressed and upset. He found that children who learned to understand and handle their feelings got along better with others and solved problems in appropriate ways. These children also had better physical health, higher academic scores, better relationships with friends, fewer behavioral problems, more positive feelings, and better emotional health. Gottman used the term "Emotion Coaching" to describe five very simple things for parents to do with children when they are emotional.[6]

Emotion Coaching requires a significant amount of commitment and patience, but the job is essentially the same as that of any other coach. If you want to see your child excel at baseball, you don't avoid the game. You get out in the yard and start working with him. Likewise, if you want to see your child handle feelings, cope with stress, and develop healthy relationships, you don't shut down or ignore expressions of negative emotion. You engage with your child and offer guidance. I will summarize this five-step emotion-coaching process.[7]

STEP 1: BE AWARE OF THE CHILD'S EMOTIONS

Children usually provide clues when something bothers them. The clues come in the form of behavior problems, a change in appetite, withdrawal from others, poor performance in school, having a sad countenance, etc. Parents should recognize these emotional clues and respond with empathy, which is the foundation of Emotion Coaching.

BRANDON'S STORY. Four-year-old Brandon entered the room to watch television with his mother and two siblings. Before sitting down, Brandon stood for a few moments in front of a chair, talking with Katie, his sister. During their conversation, Steve, an older brother, came into the room, moved the chair away from behind Brandon, and sat down. Not seeing this, Brandon proceeded to sit down but fell on the floor. The event was accidental but humorous. Everyone laughed except Brandon. Humiliated, he ran to his room, shut himself in the closet, and began weeping. Moments later his mother knocked softly and opened the door. She kneeled beside him, kissed him on the cheek, and said, "I know you're embarrassed and hurt. I'm sorry for laughing. I love you." She got up and left.

Years later, Brandon remembered the event as one of the significant moments of his childhood. Expressions of affection were rare in his family, but on this occasion he felt understood and loved at a time when he needed it most. He never forgot it.

REASONS FOR EMOTIONS. The point is, children—like all people—have reasons for their emotions, whether they can articulate those reasons or not. Whenever we find our children getting angry or upset over an issue that seems inconsequential, it may help to step back and look at the big picture of what's going on in their lives. A three-year-old can't tell you, "I'm sorry I've been so cranky lately, Mom; it's just that I've been under a lot of stress since moving to the new daycare center." An eight-year-old probably won't tell you, "I feel so tense when I hear you and dad bickering over money," but that may be what he is feeling.

When you feel your heart go out to your child, when you know you are feeling what your child is feeling, you are experiencing empathy. This is the first step in Emotion Coaching, and if you can stay with your child in this emotion—as difficult or uncomfortable as it may be—you can take the next step.

STEP 2: RECOGNIZE EMOTION AS AN OPPORTUNITY FOR CLOSENESS AND TEACHING

For many parents, recognizing children's negative emotions as opportunities for such bonding and teaching comes as a relief, a liberation, a great "aha." This step lets us look at our children's anger as something other than a challenge to our authority. Kids' fears are no longer evidence of our incompetence as parents. Their sadness doesn't have to represent just one more thing that we have to fix today.

While some parents try to ignore children's negative feelings in the hope that they will go away, emotions rarely work that way.

Instead, negative feelings dissipate when children can talk about their emotions, label them, and feel understood. If you express interest and concern over your child's broken toy or a minor scrape, these experiences are building blocks. Your child learns that you are his ally and the two of you figure out how to work together. Then if a big crisis occurs, you are prepared to face it together. Children feel understood and comforted when kind and loving parents acknowledge and understand their feelings.

KARL'S STORY. It was a beautiful, warm Saturday morning. Oscar felt happy to be alive and looked forward to spending the day with his family. After weekend chores were done, he planned on taking his children for a picnic at the city park. The family enjoyed these outings because there were so many things to do. When Oscar suggested that the children finish their work as soon as possible, he noticed that Karl, his eleven-year-old son, appeared angry. Karl looked at his father defiantly, turned around and walked off. Oscar felt surprised and concerned. Karl was a very conscientious child. Oscar asked if they could talk for a moment.

Oscar: You seemed angry when I brought up the subject of chores. Is something troubling you?

Karl: (curtly) No. I'll get them done. Don't worry about it.

Oscar: You sound upset. What's the matter?

Karl: What do you care? All you want is to get the work done, right? So, I'll get it done.

Oscar: It's true that I want the work done, but that's not all I care about. I also care about your feelings and what is bothering you. You're angry about something, and it sounds like it could be at me. I'd like to know what that's all about.

Karl: I don't like your dumb job chart—that's what's bugging me. How come my name comes up on the list to do the worst jobs more than everyone else's? It's not fair.

Oscar: Your name doesn't come up more. I made the chart so everyone does the same amount, except Meg and Annie. They're too young for the outside work.

Karl: You're wrong. I have to do more than the others.

Oscar: You think I'm being purposely unfair to you.

Karl: Yes.

Oscar: Show me what you mean. (Karl shows his father that his name is indeed on the job chart more than his two male siblings. Oscar is surprised and troubled.) You're right. I made a mistake. I'm sorry. I'll fix it right away.

Oscar changed the chart and gave his son a holiday from chores the following week. Karl was no longer angry, and good feelings soon returned.

BECOMING AN ALLY. Oscar became a true ally to his son, Karl, when he chose to see Karl's negative emotion as an opportunity for closeness and teaching. How easy it would have been for Oscar to ignore Karl's anger by simply demanding that he do the work. Instead, he was able to see the situation from Karl's point of view, which led to Oscar's realization and admission that he was the one at fault. By admitting his mistake, correcting it quickly, and giving Karl a week off chores, Oscar strengthened his relationship with Karl.

Once you can see that a situation presents an opportunity for closeness and teaching, you are ready for perhaps the most important step in the Emotion Coaching process.

STEP 3: LISTEN EMPATHETICALLY AND VALIDATE THE CHILD'S FEELINGS

This type of listening means far more than just using your ears. Empathetic listeners use their eyes to watch for physical evidence of their children's emotions. They use their imaginations to see the situation from the child's perspective. They use their words to reflect back what they are hearing. Most importantly, they use their hearts to feel what their children are feeling. Pay attention to your child's body language, sit at his level, take a deep breath, relax, and focus. Now you are ready to do some empathetic listening.

EXAMPLES OF EMPATHETIC LISTENING.

Kyle's story. When a birthday package arrived in the mail for Nicky, his four-year-old brother, Kyle, reacted with anger: "That's not fair!" Kyle protested. Typically, the boys' dad responded by explaining that, in time, it *will* be fair: "When your birthday comes, Grandma will probably send you a package, too," Dad said.

While this statement certainly explained the logic of the situation, it flatly denied how Kyle felt in the moment. Now, on top of feeling jealous about the package, Kyle probably felt angry that his dad didn't understand his unenviable position.

Imagine how differently Kyle might feel if his dad were to respond to his outburst with a simple observation: "You wish Grandma had sent you a package, too. I bet that makes you feel kind of jealous." "Yeah, that's right," Kyle might think. "Even though it's Nicky's birthday and I'm supposed to be cool about this, I feel jealous. Dad understands." Now, Kyle would be in a better spot to hear his dad's explanation that things will even out in time.

Megan's story. In the following dialogue between nine-year-old Megan and her mom, notice that the mom's first order of business is to acknowledge her daughter's feelings.

Megan: I don't want to go to school tomorrow.

Mom: You don't? That's strange. Usually you like to go to school. It makes me wonder if you're worried about something.

Megan: Yeah, kind of.

Mom: What are you worried about?

Megan: I don't know.

Mom: Something is sort of worrying you, but you're not sure what it is.

Megan: Yeah.

Mom: I can tell that you feel a little tense.

Megan: (with tears) Yeah. Maybe it's because of Dawn and Patty.

Mom: Did something happen today at school with Dawn and Patty?

Megan: Yeah. Today at recess Dawn and Patty were just ignoring me.

Mom: Oh, that must have hurt your feelings.

Megan: It did.

Mom: It sounds like you don't want to go to school tomorrow because you're worried that Dawn and Patty might ignore you at recess again.

Megan: Yeah. Every time I went up to them, they just walked away and started doing something else.

Mom: Oh, I'd feel terrible if my friends did that to me.

Megan: I did. I felt like I was going to cry.

Mom: (hugging her) Oh, honey I'm so sorry that happened to you. I can see that you feel very sad and angry about the way your friends were treating you.

Megan: I do. I don't know what to do tomorrow. I don't want to go to school.

Mom: Because you don't want your friends to hurt your feelings again.

Megan: Yeah, and that's who I always play with. Everybody else has their own friends.

The conversation continued with Megan giving her mother more details about her interaction with the girls. Several times Mom wanted to tell Megan what to do. She wanted to say things like "Don't worry. Dawn and Patty will change their tunes tomorrow," or "To heck with those girls. Find some new friends." However, Mom resisted doing this because she wanted to convey her understanding and to allow Megan to come up with some answers on her own.

If Mom had told Megan not to worry, or if she had implied there was some simple solution, she would be saying that she considered Megan's problem inconsequential or silly. Instead, Megan found a confidante in her mom and felt comforted. After several more minutes of listening and reflecting back what her daughter was telling her, Mom started exploring ideas of how to handle the situation. Because Megan knew that her mother understood her dilemma, she was receptive to her mom's advice. Here's how the rest of the conversation went:

Megan: I don't know what to do.

Mom: Do you want me to help you come up with some ideas of what you could do?

Megan: Yeah.

Mom: Maybe you could talk to Dawn and Patty about the way you feel when they ignore you.

Megan: I don't think I could. That would be too embarrassing.

Mom: Yeah, I can see why you might feel that way. That would take a lot of courage. Hmm, I don't know. Let's think. (Time passes while Mom rubs Megan's back.)

Mom: Maybe you could just wait and see what happens. You know Dawn; she can be really mean one day, but then the next day she'll be her old self again. Maybe she'll be a better friend tomorrow.

Megan: But what if she isn't?

Mom: I'm not sure. Do you have any ideas?

Megan: No.

Mom: Is there anybody else you'd like to play with?

Megan: No.

Mom: What else is happening on the playground?

Megan: Just kickball.

Mom: Do you like to play kickball?

Megan: I never played it.

Mom: Oh.

Megan: Krista always plays it.

Mom: You mean Krista, your friend from Camp Fire?

Megan: Yeah.

Mom: I've seen you with Krista at Camp Fire meetings and you're not shy around her at all. Maybe you could ask her to teach you how to play.

Megan: Maybe.

Mom: Good. Then you have another idea.

Megan: Yeah, maybe that would work. But what if it doesn't?

Mom: It seems like you're still worried. Like maybe you're afraid there just won't be anybody to play with and you won't know what to do with yourself.

Megan: Yeah.

Mom: Are there things that you can think of that are fun to play all by yourself?

Megan: You mean like jump rope?

Mom: Yeah, jump rope.

Megan: I could bring my jump rope just in case.

Mom: Yeah. Then if you don't play with Dawn and Patty, or the kickball game doesn't work out, you could play jump rope.

Megan: Yeah, I could do that.

Mom: Why don't you go put your jump rope in your backpack right now so you don't forget.

Megan: Okay. Then could I call Krista and see if she can come over after school tomorrow?

Mom: That's a great idea.

By listening empathetically, taking her time, and letting Megan come to her own conclusions, this mother was able to guide her daughter toward some workable options.

SHARE SIMPLE OBSERVATIONS. As you listen to your child in an emotional moment, be aware that sharing simple observations usually works better than using probing questions to get a conversation started. You may ask your child, "Why do you feel sad?" and she may not have a clue. Maybe she is feeling sad about her parents' arguments, or because she feels overtired, or she is worried about an upcoming piano recital. But she may or may not be able to articulate any of this and will probably clam up.

It is better to simply reflect what you notice. You can say, "You seem a little tired today," or "I noticed that you frowned when I mentioned the recital," and wait for her response. Sharing examples from your own life, when done with a humble attitude, can also be an effective way to demonstrate your understanding.

Consider the case of Kyle, the little boy who was upset over his brother's birthday present. Imagine if Dad had said, "I used to feel jealous when I was a little boy and Aunt Mary got a gift." This would assure Kyle that emotions like his are so valid that even Dad experienced them. Now that he feels understood, he can accept Dad's comforting explanation that "Grandma will probably send you a present on your birthday, too."

LISTENING GIVES CREDIBILITY TO A CHILD'S FEELINGS. When children want parents to listen to them, be careful to not respond by always giving advice. An adolescent daughter wrote her mom: "When I ask you to listen to me and you start giving advice, or telling me I shouldn't feel a certain way, or solving my problems, you aren't giving me what I've asked for. Please just listen to me. Don't talk or do."

Do you suppose that one reason prayer is so effective in people's lives is that God listens? Seldom does He give us quick fixes in prayer. Instead, He listens and from time to time gives subtle suggestions. Generally, He lets us work to solve our concerns ourselves.

Listening with understanding not only reflects back the words and the meaning of what another person is saying, it reflects what he is feeling. The feeling behind a statement is more important than the information expressed. This leads us to the next easy yet extremely important step in Emotion Coaching.

STEP 4: HELP THE CHILD IDENTIFY AND NAME EMOTIONS

We mistakenly assume that children have words to describe what they feel inside, but children do not always have a vocabulary for their emotions. Parents who provide words for children to describe feelings will help their child gain a sense of control over their emotions. Children whose feelings are often dismissed or corrected never learn the language of talking about feelings.

TODD'S STORY. Todd's parents brought him to the counselor after his most recent tantrum. They had hoped that their seven-year-old son would have outgrown his temper problem. However, the afternoon before, Todd had gone into a rage when his mother refused to take him to see his friend Brett. Todd screamed at the top of his voice, called his mother names, and kicked the wall. When the counselor asked Todd what he was feeling when his mother refused his request, he responded, "I don't know." When asked how he felt when doing the things he liked the most, he gave the same answer. Further questioning revealed that Todd had no vocabulary to express his emotions.

Todd's story may have been different if he had been able to describe his feelings clearly and accurately. Helping a child learn names that describe feelings does not guarantee the child will behave more responsibly. However, children are less likely to act out their feelings when they are able to talk about them. Also, when children describe their feelings, parents can more easily comfort and soothe emotional wounds.

TEACH FEELING WORDS IN THE EMOTIONAL MOMENT. The best time to teach feeling words is when children experience emotion. When a mother sees her daughter crying because her friend is moving away, Mother might say, "You must feel really sad. You've been such close friends." Hearing this said, the girl not only feels understood, but now she has a word that describes this intense feeling.

Labeling emotions goes hand in hand with empathy. Help your kids find words to describe what they are feeling. This doesn't mean telling kids how they *ought* to feel. It simply means helping them develop a vocabulary with which to express their emotions.

Giving credibility to children's feelings helps them understand their emotions and feel good about themselves. Once you have spent time listening to your child and helping her to label and understand her emotions, you are ready for the fifth and final step in Emotion Coaching.

STEP 5: SET LIMITS WHILE HELPING THE CHILD TO SOLVE PROBLEMS

What is a parent's role when a child gets frustrated and then expresses that negative feeling in an inappropriate way, such as hitting a playmate, breaking a toy, or name-calling? As a parent, your role is to first acknowledge the emotion behind the misbehavior and help the child to label it. Make sure the child understands that certain behaviors are inappropriate and can't be tolerated. Then guide the child into thinking of more appropriate ways to handle negative feelings.

HELPFUL EXAMPLES.

Hitting. Your child hits another child who took a toy away from him. First acknowledge and label the emotion. Next, let the child know that his behavior was not appropriate. Finally, guide him to a better way to handle the emotion.

An appropriate response may be the following: "You're mad that Danny took that game away from you. I would be, too. But it's not OK for you to hit him. What can you do instead?" Acknowledging that you would be mad, too, validates the child's feelings. This will put him in a better position to be receptive to your instruction that hitting is not an option as you work together to find an appropriate solution.

Name-calling. Your son had his heart set on riding in the front seat of the car, but his sister ran ahead of him and jumped into the front seat first. Visibly upset, he began calling her names.

Your response: "It's OK for you to feel jealous because your sister jumped into the front seat of the car before you did, but it's not OK for you to call her nasty names. Can you think of a different way to deal with your feelings?"

It is important for children to understand that their *feelings* are not the problem, their *misbehavior* is. All feelings are acceptable, but not all behaviors are. Therefore, it is the parents' job to set limits on acts, not on feelings.

REUBEN'S STORY. Reuben, age twelve, dropped a fly ball, which cost his team a win and entry in the championship playoffs. While he was walking off the field, one of his teammates shouted, "Way to go, klutz!" Already feeling horrible, Reuben ran to the youth, grabbed him around the neck and shoulders, and tried to throw him to the ground. Reuben's father immediately bolted from the stands, pulled his son away, held him firmly, and said: "I know you're angry and hurt, but we never hurt others. Let's go home and talk about a better way to handle this."

Do you see what Reuben's father did? Rather than scold or preach, he used the occasion to draw close to Reuben by listening empathetically, validating Reuben's feelings, and helping him find other ways to handle difficult situations. This helped Reuben feel understood, valued, and better able to manage his feelings.

FEELINGS DO NOT CHANGE EASILY. Remember that it is not easy for children to change the way they feel about a situation. A child's emotions of sadness, fear, or rage don't just disappear because a parent says, "Stop that crying," or "You shouldn't feel that way." If we tell a child how he *ought* to feel, it just makes him distrust what he *does* feel—a situation that leads to self-doubt and loss of self-esteem.

On the other hand, if we tell a child he has a right to his feelings—but there may be better ways to *express* those feelings—the child is left with his character and his sense of self-esteem intact. Also, he knows he has an understanding adult on his side who is going to help him go from feeling overwhelmed to finding a solution.

Recognizing, describing, and labeling feelings expressed by our children increases their self-awareness and broadens their understanding. If this is done well, a child's response will be, "That's right." "Yes, that's how I feel." The child will probably continue to talk because he feels that someone cares.

BE PATIENT WITH THE PROCESS

To be effective as an Emotion Coach, you must allow your child time to express feelings without becoming impatient. If your child is sad, he may cry. If she is angry, she may stomp her feet. It may be uncomfortable for you to spend time with your child in this state. It helps to remember that your goal is to explore and understand emotions, not to suppress them.

Acceptance and validation come from empathy—that is, feeling what your child is feeling in the moment. It is being able to say from your heart, "It *is* sad that Daddy had to leave without you." "Being hit by a friend would make *me* angry, too." "I can see that you *hate* it when I correct you."

Also, remember that you do not always need words to communicate understanding. As you sit together with an emotion, know that a hug or a back rub often says more than words—especially if the child is dealing with sadness or fear.

EXAMPLE OF JESUS CHRIST. Jesus' example as he communicated with Mary and Martha at the death of Lazarus beautifully illustrates this principle. Knowing that He would soon raise their brother from the dead, Jesus could have easily tried to comfort the grieving sisters with words explaining what was going to happen. Instead, He empathized with their emotion, sat with them through it and *wept.*[8]

WEEKLY ASSIGNMENT

At this point you must realize that once you receive a weekly assignment, it never goes away. We will simply add new dimensions to the habits you are creating to help keep these puzzle pieces in place. This week, in addition to continuing the vital practices that establish a foundation of unconditional love for your children—as well as continuing to speak the love language of your spouse—you will add the fourth piece of the parenting puzzle: Name feelings for your children and practice empathy. When your child is in an emotional moment, name the feeling you observe by stating: "You seem uneasy." "You must feel hurt." "You are very cheerful." Then spend time with the child in that emotion and show true empathy for the feelings he is experiencing.

THE MIRACLE OF THE CHINESE BAMBOO TREE

In everything you do in your family, keep in mind the miracle of the Chinese bamboo tree. After the seed for this amazing tree is planted, you see nothing, absolutely nothing, for four years except for a tiny shoot coming out of a bulb. During those four years, all the growth is underground in a massive, fibrous root structure that spreads deep and wide in the earth. But then in the fifth year the Chinese bamboo tree grows up to eighty feet!

Many things in family life are like the Chinese bamboo tree. You work and you invest time and effort, and you do everything you can possibly do to nurture growth, and sometimes you don't see anything for weeks, months, or even years. But if you're patient and keep working and nurturing, that "fifth year" will come, and you will be astonished at the growth and change you see taking place.[9]

Patience is faith in action. Patience is emotional diligence. It's the willingness to suffer inside so that others can grow. It reveals love. It gives birth to understanding.

GUIDING PRINCIPLES AND PRACTICES

This Week

NAME YOUR CHILD'S FEELINGS

PRACTICE EMPATHY

Principle #6: Feelings must be validated.
Practice #6: Practice Emotion Coaching in parent/child relationships.

Notes

1. John Gottman, *Raising an Emotionally Intelligent Child*, (New York: Simon & Schuster Paperbacks, 1997), 15-16.
2. Ibid., 31.
3. Ibid., 73.
4. Ibid., 73-74.
5. Ibid., 75.
6. Ibid., 16-17.
7. Ibid., 76-109.
8. John 11.
9. Covey, *The 7 Habits of Highly Effective Families*, 22-23.

Chapter 5
Disciplining with Love

Congratulations! By trying to be consistent in practicing the skills highlighted in each weekly assignment, you are internalizing your goal as a parent:

Proclamation-Based

EVALUATION OF NAMING YOUR CHILD'S FEELINGS AND PRACTICING EMPATHY ASSIGNMENT

Let's take a moment to revisit the sixth guiding principle and practice which was introduced in the previous chapter concerning validating feelings and emotion coaching. My fear is that you will feel about emotion coaching as I felt about CPR when it was first introduced to me. There were so many detailed steps to the process that I was sure if the need ever arose for me to practice CPR, I would totally fail. I am happy to report that current recommendations to the general public for practicing CPR have been reduced to two steps!

Unless you are a trained professional, there are only two simple steps to learn: 1) Call 911; 2) Push hard and fast on the center of the chest. This is completely doable for most of us. The main goal of CPR is to restart a heartbeat.

Similarly, do you feel there are too many detailed steps in emotion coaching for you to successfully remember? If this is true for you, let me simplify the process. The main goal of Emotion Coaching is to validate your child's feelings—whatever they may be. For this to happen you must first, notice when your child is expressing feelings and emotions—at the same time realizing that this is an opportunity for closeness—and second, name your child's feelings as you carefully listen to validate them and help guide him to appropriate behavior. Again, the main goal of Emotion Coaching is to validate your child's feelings. Remember that all feelings are acceptable and that a child can't change his feelings just because you tell him to.

As you continue to practice Emotion Coaching skills by engaging with your child in helping him to recognize and name his feelings, something incredible happens. Children who can recognize, label, and talk about their feelings in an atmosphere of acceptance are more likely to keep the commandments and to resist temptation. The child who can say, "You are making me feel very angry right now," is in a far better position to handle his feelings than the child who is unable to do so. In addition, recognizing and labeling a feeling often drains off the energy normally used in inappropriate behavior in certain situations. For example, the child who has had a favorite toy taken away by another child can meet the situation only by physical retaliation or running to an adult, unless he has learned to tell the other person what he is feeling. We will examine two more stories that illustrate the importance of naming feelings and practicing empathy.

MARK'S STORY. Eight-year-old Mark entered his room after school to change his clothes only to discover his four-year-old brother, Timmy, playing with his Legos. Angrily, Mark forcefully pushed Timmy out of the room as he shouted, "How many times have I told you to leave my Legos alone. I don't want you EVER to touch my things again!"

Timmy ran sobbing to his mother in the kitchen. Mother tried to comfort the tearful Timmy, then hurried to Mark's room and said, "Mark, you are older and know more about leaving other people's things alone than Timmy. I want you to apologize to your little brother right now." Mark stubbornly refused, replying that Timmy should not have been playing with his Legos. Mother then closed the bedroom door after telling Mark he can come out of his room when he is ready to apologize to Timmy. Mark screamed at the closed door, "I'll never come out because I'll never apologize!"

Apparently, Mark did not have the skill to tell his brother Timmy how he felt when he saw Timmy playing with his Legos. His mother became so emotionally involved in the altercation between the two boys that she too was unable to recognize the feelings of either child. She seemed more interested in the "right" behavior and ignored the feelings of both boys.

What could Mark's mom have done to handle this situation in a way that everyone wins? She could have said to the crying Timmy, "I know you wanted very much to play with Mark's Legos. But Mark is afraid you will lose them if he is not playing Legos with you because you are so young. That would make Mark very unhappy. Mark has said he would let you play Legos with him when he is home. He's feeling very angry with you right now because you played with his Legos while he wasn't here. When he is feeling less angry you may ask him to play Legos with you."

This explanation might have helped each child to recognize his own feelings and to feel less angry, because someone understood, or accepted, how he felt without accusing him of anything.

Forcing a child to apologize to another child, regardless of the provocation, may simply teach the child to deny his feelings or find another and less acceptable means to express them. In the statement, "When he is feeling less angry, you may ask him to play Legos with you," this mom could have provided an acceptable way to solve the problem for both children.[1]

MORIAH'S STORY. After visiting relatives, two-year-old Moriah was with her family on a cross-country flight home. Bored, tired, and cranky, Moriah asked her dad for Zebra, her favorite stuffed animal and comfort object. Unfortunately, her parents had absentmindedly packed the well-worn critter in a suitcase that was checked at the baggage counter.

Dad: I'm sorry, honey, but we can't get Zebra right now. He's in the big suitcase in another part of the airplane.

Moriah: (whining pitifully) I want Zebra.

Dad: I know, sweetheart. But Zebra isn't here. He's in the baggage compartment underneath the plane and Daddy can't get him until we get off the plane. I'm sorry.

Moriah: I want Zebra! I want Zebra!

Then Moriah started to cry, twisting in her safety seat and reaching futilely toward a bag on the floor where she'd seen her dad go for snacks.

Dad: (feeling his blood pressure rise) I know you want Zebra, but he's not in that bag. He's not here and I can't do anything about it. (fumbling for one of her favorite picture books) Look, why don't we read about Ernie.

Moriah: (wailing angrily) Not Ernie! I want Zebra. I want him *now!*

By now, Dad was getting "do something" looks from the passengers, from the airline attendants, from his wife, seated across the aisle. He looked at Moriah's face, red with anger, and imagined how frustrated she must feel. After all, wasn't he the guy who could whip up a peanut butter sandwich on demand? Or make huge purple dinosaurs appear with the flip of a TV switch? Now he was withholding her favorite toy from her, and he felt bad. Then it dawned on him: He couldn't get Zebra, but he could offer her the next best thing—a father's comfort.

Dad: You wish you had Zebra now.

Moriah: (sadly) Yeah.

Dad: And you're angry because we can't get him for you.

Moriah: Yeah.

Dad: You wish you could have Zebra *right now.*

Moriah stared at him, looking rather curious, almost surprised.

Moriah: Yeah. I want him *now.*

Dad: You're tired now, and smelling Zebra and cuddling with him would feel real good. I wish we had Zebra here so you could hold him. Even better, I wish we could get out of these seats and find a big, soft bed full of all your animals and pillows where we could just lie down.

Moriah: Yeah.

Dad: We can't get Zebra because he's in another part of the airplane. That makes you feel frustrated.

Moriah: (with a sigh) Yeah.

Dad: I'm so sorry.

The tension leaving her face, Moriah rested her head against the back of her safety seat. She continued to complain softly a few more times, but she was growing calmer. Within a few minutes, she was asleep.

Although Moriah was just two years old, she clearly knew what she wanted—her Zebra. Once she began to realize that getting it wasn't possible, she wasn't interested in any excuses, arguments, or diversions. Validation of her feelings, however, was another matter. Finding out that Dad understood how she felt seemed to make her feel better. Moriah's true story is a memorable testament to the power of empathy, which is the foundation of Emotion Coaching.[2]

CAUTION. Following correct principles in parenting is not a "quick fix." **Be patient.** Remember the miracle of the Chinese Bamboo Tree: The "fifth year" will come!

"Come Unto Me" Relationship Reminders

- ♥ Understand child development
- ♥ Listen to understand
- ♥ Be kind
- ♥ Show empathy

The parent/child relationship level of the Parenting Pyramid is extremely important to have in place before moving to the next level. Good communication is essential in family relationships and involves all four elements of the "Come Unto Me" relationship listed above.

Words and behavior have the power to hurt or to help, to inflict pain and suffering or to soothe painful feelings, to provoke doubt and fear or to instill faith and courage. Parents are skilled at different levels, but ultimately, it's not the skill that's important. It is the sincerity of parents' hearts to really want to know what their child's world is like.

If we as parents are going to be good listeners, we must be prepared to hear things we don't want to hear. We must be prepared to hear our children try out a new idea, or to say they don't agree with us, or they don't like something that we like. Otherwise, they are going to quickly learn that "I can't really say how I'm thinking or how I'm feeling." Communication comes when people feel like they really are heard and that what they are saying counts and is important.

WARNING. The first step in improving communication is to recognize when a change needs to be made and be persistent in making the change. When parents try something new with their children, two things happen. First, children test parents to see if they will stick to what they are doing. Parents sometimes struggle with the pull of their own habits, and they find out how difficult it can be to change patterns they have used for years. Second, homeostasis comes into play. Homeostasis is the body's tendency to stay the same, to snap back when there is a change. The problem is that homeostasis works to keep things the same even if "the same" is not very good. It takes courage to stay on the path and perhaps to change some long-time parenting patterns.

TEACHING

With the parent/child relationship level in place, we are now ready for the teaching level of the pyramid. Our discussion on teaching will begin with a definition of discipline. Discipline comes from the word *disciple*, which means to follow. An appropriate synonym for discipline is training or teaching. Discipline is training a child in the way he should go in two areas: 1) Training to develop orderly conduct or proper behavior; 2) Training to develop self-control and responsibility.

The prophet Joseph Smith taught early saints correct principles and let them govern themselves.[3] As parents, we can do the same for our children. Proper discipline is an excellent means of teaching self-control and responsible behavior, but it is also one of the hardest challenges we face. If parents don't have a specific, deliberate plan for discipline, they are likely to rely on instinct and react emotionally to each situation. Part of this specific plan should be to make a conscious decision to support one another.

No training can be truly effective if both parents do not agree on the method of disciplining. Dallin H. Oaks has taught: "The father presides and has the ultimate responsibility in the government of the home, but parenting is obviously a shared responsibility. Both parents occupy a leading role in teaching their children, and both must counsel together and support one another."[4]

To be unified, couples must spend time together discussing ideas and planning approaches. Perhaps spending a weekend away together a few times a year to have this discussion and to plan their approaches would help a couple become unified in feelings and objectives. Sometimes you may disagree with the way your spouse handles a problem with one of your children. The best thing to do in this situation is to support your spouse in front of the child and discuss the problem later with your spouse in private.

HOW DOES LOVE RELATE TO DISCIPLINE?

Love and discipline cannot be separated. The first fact to understand in order to have a well-disciplined child is that making a child feel loved is the first and most important part of good discipline.[5] First things first—practice unconditional love then discipline. Discipline is immeasurably easier when a child feels unconditionally loved. Without unconditional love, a child will react to guidance with anger, hostility, and resentment. It is a true statement that "If you love your child, you must discipline your child." The problem is not whether to discipline. Providing discipline is our responsibility as parents. The problem is how to manifest love to a child through discipline.

Often, discipline is confused with punishment, as though the two were synonymous. As a young mother, I believed that discipline and punishment *were* synonyms. They are *not*. Discipline is positive guidance to good behavior, a way of communicating values to a child. Punishment is inflicting something negative upon a child for poor behavior. There is little to be learned positively from being grounded, spanked, placed on a chair, or yelled at for doing wrong.

WHY DO WE PUNISH?

Punishment is done mainly for the parent. Inflicting a punishment gives parents a feeling that they are doing something, and there is often an immediate reward—the undesirable behavior stops. We have all been informally taught how to look for mistakes and how to punish. Most of us, however, have little training in how to look for what people are doing right or how to reward good behavior, such as complimenting for doing a good job on homework, praising for doing a chore without being asked, showing you notice and appreciate a child's efforts to be responsible. Recognizing and rewarding good behavior is more effective than punishing bad behavior. In most cases, if a child receives enough unconditional love and loving discipline, punishment will not be necessary.[6]

THE BOSTON FERN STORY. One of best illustrations I have found of the difference between punishment and discipline is described by Layne E. Flake in his story of the Boston fern:

> The long, cold winter in upstate New York had begun to take its toll on everyone's nerves. We had been practically confined to the house for five months. One day, our eleven-year-old son, Taylor, decided to use the living room as a basketball court, and in the

process broke every branch of our struggling Boston fern.

Faced with the dilemma, his mother could follow the natural inclination to hide the basketball for two weeks, send Taylor to his room for the evening, and broadcast our displeasure. Or she could discuss with him the consequences of disobeying a family rule and arrange for him to replace the plant. The contrast in approaches is the difference between *punishment* and *discipline.*[7]

Punishment is directed at the child; it is done *to* the child. "Go to your room!" Discipline is directed at the child's behavior; it is done *for* the child. "Come unto me." True discipline is not emotionally charged, whereas, punishment is frequently accompanied by uncontrolled emotions such as anger.

One of this week's assignments will be to evaluate where your responses to your children fall—punishment or discipline? Now that we have a better understanding of discipline, let's look at two more essentials on this level of the pyramid.

TWO ESSENTIALS: RELATIONSHIPS AND RULES—IN THAT ORDER

Relationships must be firmly established before any type of rules can be put into place. For this reason, we have spent the first few chapters of this book discussing relationships. Now we will examine the necessity of rules.

Order is an Eternal Principle. The principle of order is an important characteristic of the kingdom of God. "Behold, mine house is a house of order, saith the Lord God..." (Doctrine and Covenants 133:8). One way the Lord maintains order in His kingdom is to bless those who obey certain laws. "There is a law, irrevocably decreed in heaven before the foundations of this world, upon

> *Order is an Eternal Principle.*

which all blessings are predicated—And when we obtain any blessing from God, it is by obedience to that law upon which it is predicated" (Doctrine and Covenants 130:20- 21).

An orderly home also operates upon this important principle. Family rules must be established and observed *before* the blessing of family harmony can be attained. Rules are used to discern obedience from disobedience. We teach disobedience when we fail to enforce rules. The Lord holds parents responsible to have children account to them.

OBEDIENCE: THE FIRST LAW OF HEAVEN. Obedience should not be mistaken for conformity. True obedience requires the exercise of agency knowing that good will come from obeying. In contrast, conformity is merely compliance because of pressure to do so. To be truly obedient, a person must go beyond merely conforming. Obedience includes agency, knowledge of God's laws, and motivation to live the laws.

There are times when we *must* make children obey. However, if this is all we do, we remove their freedom with our pressure. Yet, with too little pressure, they may not obey at all. How then do we motivate children to *choose* to obey? We motivate them with our adaptable approach to family rules and by teaching them to participate in a relationship with us to increase their agency.[8]

THE LESSER LAW VERSUS THE HIGHER LAW. Rules in a family operate on two different levels. First, we have the lesser law, which governs actions. We see an example of the lesser law in the Law of Moses. This collection of rules was given through Moses to govern a person's outward actions rather than inner thoughts and motives. Our family laws are the lesser law that governs the outward actions of people in the family. Next is the higher law, which governs spiritual growth. The Savior's gospel of love represents the higher law. His gospel introduced the Holy Ghost, which speaks to the spiritual part of us. Relationships become the higher law in the family.

If exclusive attention is given to external behavior and actions (e.g., "Is your work done?" "Stop acting that way!") and rules are formed to regulate it, children may acquire only the qualities like many Pharisees. There will be outward conformity but no internal growth. On the other hand, if we increase our focus to include internal conditions where the gospel suggests we should, we set the stage for inner growth and relationships to develop to a higher level.[9]

CHILDREN AND THEIR RULES

There is no such thing as a family without rules. Any regular event is a family rule. It may be informal, like a family tradition, or formal, like getting dressed before breakfast. Anything repeated often enough becomes a rule, and there are differences in the number of informal and formal rules. Informal rules evolve naturally as a part of family living. Formal rules are taught to children and enforced.

A crucial principle for parents to understand is that the concept children have about rules changes as they mature. In fact, children's acceptance of parental authority depends on whether parents match their use of rules to a child's stage of development. For any plan of discipline to succeed, parents need to understand the stages of rule development and be able to adapt rules to a child's individual level of maturity.

STAGES OF RULE DEVELOPMENT. The chart below provides a diagram of the development of children's concepts about rules. A discussion of each stage follows:

Development of Children's Concepts About Rules

Stage	Age	Children's Stage	Parent's Actions	Pitfalls
#1	0-4	No formal concept of rules	Caretakers and Teachers	Structuring and harshly enforcing rules
#2	4-10	Rigid concept of rules	Teachers and enforcers	Irregularity in teaching and enforcing rules
#3	10-13	Begin to adapt rules	Explainers and negotiators	Enforcing too many or too few rules
#4	13-18	Ability to formulate own rules	Teachers of principles	Enforcing rules as we would at younger ages

Stage #1: Prior to three and a half years of age, a child has no concept of formal rules. Thus, parents do not need to worry about formal rules during the first years of a child's life. Instead, they must simply involve children in many informal rules or routines. The main job of a parent during this stage is to provide basic care for their children and to keep them safe.

A father made this observation one day:

> Our young son, a toddler, climbed inside the pots-and-pans cupboard and threw them out on the floor, enjoying the clanging sounds. I removed him from that affair, and before I finished gathering the pans, I heard him on the dining room table, throwing things off of it. I lifted him from the table and began lifting the chairs up to prevent him from climbing up again. Before I could finish this, I heard noises from my home office and quickly went to see; I found him on my desk throwing books and papers off. I felt as though a good spanking would help me feel better. But by then I had learned it wouldn't have made much difference to him, so I hugged him and gave him a new toy. He never repeated the wrong action.[10]

The pitfall for parents to avoid in stage one is attempting to structure and harshly enforce rules. Attempts to create formal rules to regulate children of this age often end in failure.

Stage #2: From four years to nine, a child forms a concept of formal rules that is fairly rigid and inflexible. They prefer life to be organized and predictable. This is a crucial time for parents to identify a few basic rules, such as what chores children are responsible for and how children should act, including showing politeness and respect. Parents must teach by example, showing children what is expected and consistently following through by reinforcing success with positive consequences and failure with encouragement to keep practicing.

President David O. McKay taught that the best time for the child to learn rules of obedience is between the ages of three and five. "If mother does not get control of the child during those ages, she will find great difficulty in getting control later. …I do not mean to push and drag or confine—just let the little child be perfectly free to develop until he goes beyond the bounds of safety. Then let him feel the gentle but firm hand of restraint."[11]

The pitfall to avoid in stage two is for parents to lack regularity in teaching and enforcing rules. Lack of consistency by parents in this area may cause children to be less secure and more difficult to manage.

Stage #3: Children in the ten to twelve age range show an inclination to adapt rules to fit their circumstances. Therefore, they expect that rules and their enforcement should be logical and understandable. As parents, you will need to increase your explanations and reasons for rules and expect children to try to negotiate with you.

The story of Karl and the job chart in the previous chapter is a good illustration of this principle. As an eleven-year-old, Karl felt his job assignments were not as logical as he expected. Fortunately, his dad was able to negotiate the situation with Karl to produce a positive outcome.

The pitfall to be avoided by parents in stage three is enforcing too many or too few rules. Now is the time to begin to de-emphasize formal rules and to clarify what to do in specific situations.

Stage #4: In the last stage of child development, beginning around age thirteen, children have the ability to formulate their own rules to fit their own purposes. This necessitates the need to replace the emphasis on formal rules with the creation of a positive parent-child relationship. Such a relationship allows discussion of what is best in each situation, clarifies what each expects, and allows the child to govern himself. To state it another way: Children's conduct is regulated through their relationship with their parents.

> *Children's conduct is regulated through their relationship with their parents.*

The pitfall to be avoided in stage four is attempting to enforce rules the same way we would for younger children. Rules become principles which children apply by themselves based on previous rules they have learned and the requirements of a new situation.[12]

THE GOVERNING RELATIONSHIP: HOW RULES BECOME PRINCIPLES

In order for children to develop a sense of freedom that permits obedience, they must gradually learn how to act without much authority imposed upon them. They must be able to think more thoroughly and adapt rules to fit several situations. As parents, we need something which gradually changes us from the position of enforcer of rules to a teacher of principles for living. This is done in the establishment of a positive parent-child relationship which emphasizes relations with one another instead of reward or punishment of children.

Most child discipline techniques emphasize ways to enforce rules in order to manage what children do. We tend to overlook the extraordinary influence of the relationship between parent and child. If the relationship has the proper ingredients, it is much more effective in teaching children to correctly apply principles than any system of rules we could devise.

FOUR PROPER INGREDIENTS OF A GOVERNING RELATIONSHIP:

1) Each person is considered equally important. Although they may each act differently and may each have different ideas based on their unique life experience, they are on the same team.

2) Frequent communication. Parent and child tell each other their feelings and ideas and keep each informed about activities.

Specifically, they tell each other their plans and inform one another if those plans change.

3) Freedom and trust. As parents and children, we say what we will do, and we do what we say.

4) Expression of love. A governing relationship is based on encouraging love. Love that is expressed to each other reinforces the value and the influence of the relationship.[13]

HOW TO SET FAMILY RULES

Effective families have few but specific rules. There are two things to remember about family rules. First, take time to set rules. Second, make sure the rules are understood by the children. Here is an example of five basic family rules:

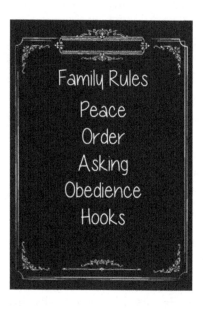

PEACE. The rule of peace includes things ranging from "No Fighting, No Biting," to no loud words, anger, or screaming. Anything that invites peace into your home is embraced by this rule, whereas things that detract from peace are prohibited.

ORDER. Order covers leaving rooms in order, taking out only one toy at a time, and putting away things that you use. It promotes taking responsibility for your own messes and not creating more work for others.

ASKING. This means never going somewhere without asking first or using something that belongs to someone else without asking for their permission.

OBEDIENCE. Minding mother and father defines this rule. Part of obedience is always showing respect to parents and other family members.

HOOKS. Hooks happens to be a method to keep track of chores to be done. Each child has "hooks" with various family jobs, practicing, etc., hanging on each hook. As the tasks are completed, they are turned over on the hook.[14]

Another of your assignments for the week will be to evaluate your family rules. Do you have family rules? Are they working? Do they need to be revamped? What changes need to be made? When will you make changes? How will you teach your children about rules?

Decide on your rules as a family. However, don't assume that once rules are in place that your children will turn into lovely obedient angels overnight. These principles are true and they work, but not without much effort. Obedience in children doesn't develop overnight, especially when children are not used to the idea of following laws and being obedient. You may have to have twenty-five Family Home Evening lessons to discuss laws. The point is, teaching obedience is not easy and can't be done in one or two easy lessons. Don't be discouraged. Persevere! Practice! It will make you happy, and it will make your children happy. Children really do love to obey!

GOOD PARENTS CHANGE THEMSELVES FIRST

Teaching discipline to children requires parents to discipline themselves. Changes must begin with us not our children. In fact, being a good parent is more about changing ourselves than about changing our children.

The Natural Parent

is an Enemy to Children

When we focus more on our own need to learn and grow than our children's, our children will benefit. As we become better people, we become better parents.

WEEKLY ASSIGNMENT

This week's puzzle piece will involve making two important internal evaluations while continuing to practice outward vital skills we have learned. First, evaluate your responses to your children. Do you respond with punishment or discipline? Second, evaluate your family rules and formulate a plan to help them succeed.

GUIDING PRINCIPLES AND PRACTICES

Principle #7: Order is necessary.

Principle #8: Relationships come before rules; unconditional love comes before discipline.

Practice #7: Establish and enforce family rules.

Practice #8: Build and maintain a "Come Unto Me" relationship with children.

This Week

EVALUATE YOUR RESPONSES:
PUNISHMENT OR DISCIPLINE!

EVALUATE YOUR FAMILY
RULES!

Notes
1. Barbara Vance, "How Children Learn to Behave," *Ensign*, May 1973, 37-40.
2. Gottman, *Raising an Emotionally Intelligent Child*, 69-70.
3. *Teachings of the Presidents of the Church: Joseph Smith* (2007), 284.
4. Dallin H. Oaks, "Parental Leadership in the Family," *Ensign*, June 1985, 9.
5. Campbell, *How to Really Love Your Child*, 86.
6. Ibid., 92.
7. Layne E. and Jana Squires Flake, "Punishment—or Discipline," *Ensign*, Oct. 1983, 39.
8. A. Lynn Scoresby, *In the Heart of a Child*, (Salt Lake City: Bookcraft, 1987), 39.
9. Ibid., 41.
10. Ibid., 42-43.
11. Handbook for Families, "Teaching Children to Govern Themselves," *Ensign*, June 1986, 36.
12. Scoresby, *In the Heart of a Child*, 42-47.
13. Ibid., 48-49.
14. Linda and Richard Eyre, *Teaching Children Responsibility*, (Salt Lake City: Deseret Book, 1982), 39.

Chapter 6
Teaching Responsibility

D iane was already late for work as she tried to coax three-year-old Joshua into his jacket so she could take him to daycare. After a too-quick breakfast and a battle over which shoes to wear, Joshua was tense too. He didn't really care that his mom had a meeting in less than an hour. He wanted to stay home and play, he told her. When Diane told him that wasn't possible, Joshua fell to the floor. Feeling sad and angry, he started to cry.[1]

Does anyone reading this chapter relate to the above scenario? It may not be that you are late for work and daycare, but just that you are late for any appointment or plans, and your child starts to behave as Joshua did that morning. What's a parent to do? You have learned some correct principles that should apply, yet you also feel the power of homeostasis—your body wants to snap back to its old way of doing things, though you know the old way is not what you want. Yes, it takes courage to stay on the path and perhaps to change some parenting patterns that have not been positive.

Proclamation-Based

A crucial reminder about communication at this point: You cannot not communicate. All communication should be done in kindness as you seek to effectively express unconditional love to your child, constantly working on a "Come Unto Me" relationship. Take a deep breath and pray for the gift of charity.

What are Diane's options with Joshua? She might dismiss his feelings altogether and distract him by bribing him with a cookie. She might scold him and threaten to spank him. She might even embrace Joshua, empathize with him, and make a deal to play a game with him for ten minutes—then it's out the door with no crying. Until tomorrow morning, that is. If Diane can practice correct principles, perhaps the conversation would go something like this:

Diane: Let's put on your jacket, Joshua. It's time to go.

Joshua: No! I don't want to go to daycare.

Diane: You don't want to go? Why not?

Joshua: Because I want to stay here with you.

Diane: You do?

Joshua: Yeah, I want to stay home.

Diane: Gosh, I think I know just how you feel. Some mornings I wish you and I could just curl up in a chair and look at books together instead of rushing out the door. But you know what? I made an important promise to the people at my office that I'd be there by nine o'clock and I can't break that promise.

Joshua: (starting to cry) But why not? It's not fair. I don't want to go.

Diane: Come here, Josh. (taking him onto her lap) I'm sorry, honey, but we can't stay home. I'll bet that makes you feel disappointed, doesn't it?

Joshua: (nodding) Yeah.

Diane: And kind of sad?

Joshua: Yeah.

Diane: I feel kind of sad, too. (She lets him cry for a while and continues to hug him, letting him have his tears.) I know what we can do. Let's think about tomorrow, when we don't have to go to work and daycare. We'll be able to spend the whole day together. Can you think of anything special you'd like to do tomorrow?

Joshua: Have pancakes and watch cartoons?

Diane: Sure, that would be great. Anything else?

Joshua: Can we take my wagon to the park?

Diane: I think so.

Joshua: Can Kyle come, too?

Diane: Maybe. We'll have to ask his mom. But right now it's time to get going, okay?

Joshua: Okay.

Marvelous! Do you recognize the critical things that Diane did to turn this difficult situation into a positive experience? Not only did she acknowledge her son's sadness and help him to name it, she also allowed him to experience his feelings and stayed with him while he cried. She didn't try to distract his attention away from his feelings. Nor did she scold him for feeling sad. Diane let Joshua know that she respected his feelings and thought his wishes were valid. Finally, she showed him that it was possible to move beyond his sad feelings and look forward to fun the next day.[2]

EVALUATION OF PUNISHMENT VS. DISCIPLINE AND FAMILY RULES ASSIGNMENT

Let's do a quick review of the difference between discipline and punishment. Discipline is directed at the *behavior* and is positive guidance to good behavior, whereas, punishment is directed at the *child* and involves inflicting something negative for poor behavior. Put another way, discipline is done *for* the child, and punishment is done *to* the child. Did you discern which you were using this week?

Through punishment a parent controls a child's actions.

Through good discipline a parent teaches a child to control his own actions.[3]

Our reason for disciplining children is to help them humble their hearts and repent of their sins because we know this is what will bring lasting happiness. In other words, if children have hardened their hearts and are doing something wrong, they must be helped to humble themselves and thus receive the spirit of the Lord, which is our main purpose for providing discipline to our children. If that is our purpose, we will not make many mistakes in discipling our children.[4] If our purpose is any other—such as to bring attention to ourselves for the proper behavior of our children—parenting will be a confusing, frustrating burden.

Remember to have a positive philosophy about the basic nature of children. Children are innately good. A parent's job is to guide behavior using the gentlest way possible. The relationship between parents and children must be in order. It is not enough for parents to feel good about their children. Children must also feel good about their parents. Then the discipline will work.

Family rules are another thing that will work only after relationships are in order. If you want success in a game, you must have rules to follow. The same is true of family life. Do you have family rules in place? Don't forget to match your use of rules to your child's stage of development. Your job changes through each stage: First, keeping the child safe; second, teaching nonstop and consistently following through; third, de-emphasizing rules by clarifying situations; fourth, creating a positive parent/child relationship, or governing relationship. The governing relationship is our goal as a parent. In this type of relationship, children's conduct is regulated through their relationship with their parents. Together they discuss what is best in each situation and clarify what each expects. The child is then allowed to govern himself.

At this point you must be asking, "What is the consequence for breaking a family rule?" Although this will be covered more completely when we reach the top level of the pyramid, the consequence for breaking a rule may simply be talking to the child about it and giving him the opportunity to keep practicing.

TEACH CHILDREN HOW TO WORK

An essential part of teaching children responsibility is teaching them how to work. Brigham Young taught: "Each one will find that happiness in this world mainly depends on the work he does, and the way in which he does it."[5] Neal A. Maxwell offers this timely advice:

> I do not believe people can be happy unless they have work to do. One can really be more of a slave to idleness than to work. Work also keeps us humble and reminds us of how all our blessings come to us from our Heavenly Father.

The gospel of work is a very important teaching of the Church. If we learn to work early in life we will be better individuals, better members of families, better neighbors, and better disciples of Jesus Christ, who Himself learned to work as a carpenter.[6]

One of the best things you can do for your children is to organize their work—at toddler age. *This* is what helps them to become responsible. Elder Maxwell wisely warns, "Those who do too much *for* their children will soon find they can do nothing *with* their children."[7] Joe J. Christensen further warns that overindulging children weakens them and takes away from them the blessing of anticipating, of longing for something they do not have. He cautions that children must learn to work, or they will leave home ill-prepared for the outside world.[8]

SIX PRINCIPLES FOR TEACHING CHILDREN TO WORK

Home is like an apprentice shop where children learn skills, habits, responsibility, dependability and self-discipline. It is especially important that children are trained to develop self-discipline. Making a bed is not a difficult skill to learn. The challenge lies in making it *every* day! Children who gain mastery over little things, such as making beds, will have power over greater things.[9]

PRINCIPLE #1: GIVE CHILDREN AN INCENTIVE. Everyone works better with incentives. Wise parents provide incentives for children until they are mature enough to establish incentives of their own. You will usually have to use a great variety of incentives, but this will help children build habits and values so that one day they will be self-motivated and self-disciplined. Here are some examples of appropriate incentives for children:

- ✓ When the dishes are done, we will bake cookies.
- ✓ When the weeds are pulled, we will go swimming.
- ✓ When the toys are picked up and you are ready for bed, we will read a story.

  ✓ When your homework is finished, we will play ball.
  ✓ When your practicing is done, we will go shopping together.

Be mindful that you do not confuse incentives with bribes. "When the weeds are pulled, we will go swimming" is an incentive. "If you pull the weeds, I will take you swimming" is a bribe. Choose your words carefully to ensure that you convey the correct message to your children.

A good example of how to use incentives is found in the Saturday work apron. This multi-pocketed apron is donned by a parent on Saturday morning as the children begin their morning jobs. As each child completes his or her jobs, they are awarded the opportunity to choose an incentive from one of the pockets. Incentives range from small toys and treats to notes promising a game to be played or a book to be read with Mom or an ice cream cone or a lunch out with Dad. Keep the incentives simple for you but motivating for your children!

PRINCIPLE #2: MAKE WORK FUN FOR CHILDREN. Making work fun for children starts with your positive attitude. Incorporate a "Mary Poppins mindset" into your family jobs: "In every job that must be done there is an element of fun. You find the fun and—snap—the job's a game!"

Meet "Gunny Bag," a simple drawstring bag with a face and a big mouth who "eats" toys that are not in their proper place. He comes complete with his own catchy, rhythmic tune, which quickly becomes lodged in your brain. Once you have introduced Gunny and his song to your children, they will squeal and scramble to clean up toys when they hear, "Here comes Gunny Bag…Yum Yummy Yummy…He eats left-over toys and keeps um in his tummy." The toys eaten by Gunny Bag may either be "coughed up" on a designated day to then be put away, or they may be purchased by the owner for a small fee. Use your imagination![10]

PRINCIPLE #3: MAKE WORK EASY FOR CHILDREN. Do not just tell children to *do* a job—show them *how* to do it! You may have to help a two or three-year-old make the bed every morning for several years, but by the age of five, making the bed has become a habit. Give children a table-setting template to help them practice setting the table. Move your dishes to the lower shelves in your kitchen to allow children to unload a dishwasher with ease.

Take time to really train children to clean a bathroom, work in the kitchen, bake cookies, sweep a floor, or care for the yard. Performing a task is easy if you know how!

PRINCIPLE #4: BE CONSISTENT IN REQUIRING CHILDREN'S HELP. Almost without fail, Billy came to the dinner table every night with dirty hands and face and would be sent to wash. One day mother asked in frustration, "Billy, why do you always come to the table without washing? You know I'll send you away to wash." Billy explained, "Well, once you forgot."

Children should be used to similar responsibilities every day. If you required them to help yesterday but not today, don't be surprised when they argue if you ask for help tomorrow. Decide what you expect of your children and stick to it. A reasonable expectation is to have a child do some type of kitchen work as well as housework each day.

Let's consider some chore-related expectations according to children's ages and stages of development:

Toddlers. Very young children are eager to help—so let them! Unless a task is dangerous or destructive, let the child have the fun and growth which comes from trying.

Preschoolers. At this stage the child must be motivated before he will work. Incentives play a major role in encouraging a preschooler to work.

Ages 6-11. Children of this age give the best help around the house. This is the age to train them to be effective in their responsibilities and make certain that proper work habits are being formed.

Teens. Older children and teens are so busy with studies, jobs, and social activities that they don't have as much time to help around the house as they did when they were younger. They are out doing the things you have prepared them for! However, even the busiest teen should keep his own room in order and should not make work for someone else through sloppiness or inconsideration.

PRINCIPLE #5: ORGANIZE CHILDREN'S WORK FOR THEM. When work is organized and systemized it can be accomplished in half the time. Even a young child appreciates this! Choose a method that works for whatever stage your family is in and realize that methods will change as your family changes. So, try them all—charts, wheels, lists, hooks, pegs; methods don't matter. The relationship is the key!

PRINCIPLE #6: LET CHILDREN FEEL APPRECIATION FOR THEIR EFFORTS. Children will do almost anything for a parent's smile, approval, or sincere thanks. Don't forget to express appreciation to your children.

Remember: It takes *years* of teaching, training, showing patience, diligence, understanding, and encouragement—along with lots and lots of follow-up—to really prepare a child to be a good worker. Look forward to the miracle of the Chinese bamboo tree. Your assignment this week will be to evaluate your children's work.

OUR HOMES MUST BE CORRECT MODELS FOR RESPONSIBLE BEHAVIOR

Proclamation-based parenting gives parents the sacred duty to teach children. Since the world offers all sorts of models for *irresponsible* behavior, we must make our homes the correct models for *responsible* behavior.

All successful and enduring institutions possess three elements:

1) Rules or laws (a legal system)
2) A way of allocating resources (an economy)
3) Strong traditions based on shared values

For our families to be successful and enduring institutions, they must also possess the same three elements:

 1) A legal system: fair, consistent, discipline-based rules and limits

 2) An economy: a way for children to earn, save, and spend money

3) Traditions and values: family activities that build communication, trust, and togetherness

Every home has these three elements—consciously or unconsciously developed. If these elements are haphazard or unconsciously developed, this is what our family institution will look like: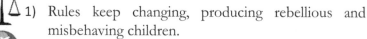

1) Rules keep changing, producing rebellious and misbehaving children.

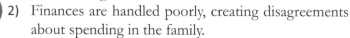 2) Finances are handled poorly, creating disagreements about spending in the family.

3) No traditions develop, causing the family to drift apart

It takes time and conscious effort to implement these elements in a family. Therefore, we must know *why* we are doing it to give us motivation and incentive to stick to it. Why should we want to put time and effort into implementing these elements in our family? Simply because having these elements in place **prepares our children for the real world:**

1) Children will have laws to obey.
2) If children are not taught to earn, they will expect something for nothing.
3) If there are no traditions to look forward to, children will enter adulthood without good memories, good habits, or good values

Since we have already discussed the legal system of the family—creating family rules—we will next explore how a family allocates resources.

THE FAMILY ECONOMY

What does children's work have to do with the family's economy? There are many differing opinions on whether to pay children for working at home. Some feel it is expected for children to share in home responsibilities because they are part of the family. On the other hand, freedom in the use of a fixed allowance or income is an excellent tool for teaching responsibility. The child who is given money whenever he needs it is not learning responsible behavior. If, however, he is able to earn a certain amount each week to spend as he pleases—and he knows that he must meet certain expenses out of that money—he will be more likely to budget and control his expenses.

Children must be able to earn money first, to be taught the principle of tithing (pay the Lord first); second, to be taught the principle of saving (pay yourself next); third, to be taught the principle of spending (live within your means). How will children earn money if we don't pay them for doing their jobs? Great question—one that I asked myself more than once while in the throes of parenting young children. The solution I discovered was a system we named the "Family Bank."[11] Let me explain.

SHIFTING THE INITIATIVE TO CHILDREN. Parents can usually get their kids to do things if they (the parents) stay right on top of them (the kids) and push them to practice, to do their jobs, and to take care of their things. Sound familiar? What is needed is a system that shifts the initiative from the parents to the children. Could it be putting stickers on a chart or having regular goal-setting sessions with children? Could it be leaving things undone and letting children suffer the natural consequences? My answer to these questions is "Been there—done that"—and it didn't work, at least not for me. What *did* work for me was a system where the children shared household responsibilities and had weekly paydays instead of weekly allowance days.

THE FAMILY BANK. Here is an example of one way to set up a Family Economy using the Family Bank. As I share this system, please realize that each family should tailor-make its own system according to the unique personalities and situations in the family. Our Family Bank system was an adaptation of an idea I read about when our children were ages 14, 13, 11, 8, 7, and 3. It did not succeed overnight but took lots of discussion and some trial and error before it was fully operational. Remember that family patterns take time to establish, but once patterns are in place, they will save time.

"Things I GET to do." This was the title of our children's weekly lists. Over the years we used a variety of methods to keep track of family jobs. The list method is the one we used in connection with the Family Bank. Truthfully, the method does not matter as long as the relationship between parents and children is in place. Use the method that works best for your family. The sample list illustrates that each child had five things to do each day: 1) Morning routines of personal grooming, making bed, etc.; 2) Practice the piano; 3) Daily schoolwork; 4) One housework job; 5) One kitchen job. Saturday work included the five basics plus some additional "Saturday jobs." We used this version of our list when only two children remained at home. Earlier versions of the list included more jobs for housework to choose from. The idea is to match the number of jobs to be done to the number of children to do the jobs.

Things I GET to do:

	Mon	Tues	Wed	Thur	Fri	Sat
Make bed, etc.						
Practice						
Schoolwork						
Housework:						
__Sweep kitchen						
__Sweep porch						
Kitchen Work:						
__Clear/Wash/Counters						
__Load/Unload/Set						

Saturday only:
Clean bathroom
Put away tub
Vacuum: __Upstairs or __Downstairs
Housework: __Mop kitchen/Prints & Microwave
__Wastebaskets/Sweep back patio

Points. As the five basic tasks are completed each day, the kids mark off the box. Each marked box is worth 25 points, making 125 points possible per day and 750 possible points per week. Any child who earns all possible points is rewarded by having his points doubled to 1500! Saturday jobs earn an additional 100 points, bringing the total possible points to 1600. If a child wants to earn extra make-up points, there are always "extra" jobs available to be done if he asks for that opportunity.

Payday. On Sunday during Family Council, the points are totaled, and each child is paid a penny per point. With cash in hand, children

can now pay the Lord first (10% tithing), pay themselves next (10% savings), and deposit the balance into the Family Bank. (Our Family Bank is a simple wooden box, which fits nicely in a cupboard above our kitchen desk.) Children keep their own personal deposit records, and the "banker" (Dad) keeps a master ledger of all deposits as well.

Responsible Spending. With their own "earned money," kids now have the responsibility to buy their own clothes, personal items, and entertainment experiences. When they need cash during the week, they retrieve it from the Family Bank and sign for the amount they withdraw. If they go shopping with a parent who buys an item for them, the receipt for the item is placed in the Family Bank. All accounts are settled and adjusted accordingly each week during Family Council. This system doesn't require any additional money. Parents are simply taking the funds they spend on children anyway and channeling that money through the kids who "earn it" and make their own purchase decisions.

Final word. Two items we continued to purchase for our children were underwear and socks—things that probably would never have made it on their "must have" list. Since the age of accountability is eight years old, this is the age when we included children to participate fully in the Family Bank system. The younger children still had their lists and were a part of our Family Council, but they were paid on a much lower scale, according to their understanding. The beauty of this system is that you can alter the number and value of points children earn according to your individual budget and circumstance. As a personal testimonial, let me say that it was a huge blessing in our family—a way to teach correct principles to our children and to let them govern themselves.

With an understanding of the first two elements of successful and enduring institutions—Family Rules and Family Economy—we are now ready to discuss the third element.

TEACHING CHILDREN TRADITIONS AND VALUES

Children will learn values in a variety of settings—at school, in the neighborhood—but home is going to be the foundation of that. Gordon B. Hinckley taught:

> When all is said and done, the primary place in building a value system is in the homes of the people. It is not enough simply to provide food and shelter for the physical being. There is an equal responsibility to provide nourishment and direction to the spirit and the mind and the heart.
>
> The health of any society, the happiness of its people, their prosperity, and their peace all find their roots in the teaching of children by fathers and mothers.[12]

Parents should be the master teachers of their children. The Church will assist parents in their teaching and training, but only assist. The Church cannot be a substitute for parental responsibility. Of this responsibility, James E. Faust stated, "To have successful homes, values must be taught; and there must be rules, there must be standards, and there must be absolutes."[13] Where do we find values, rules, standards, and absolutes? These essentials are found in the Gospel of Jesus Christ.

It is the tremendous privilege of parents to teach their children what they believe. These truths must be taught in the home. They cannot be taught in the public schools. They will not be fostered by government or society. Church programs can help, but the most effective teaching takes place in the home.

WHAT TO TEACH. Does a curriculum exist for instructing parents in what to teach their children? Fortunately, there are some inspired principles directed to parents found in Doctrine and Covenants section 68. Verses 25-26 specifically direct parents to teach children the doctrines of faith, repentance, baptism, and the gift of the Holy Ghost. Children need to be able to understand and to recognize the influence of the Holy Ghost in their lives. Teach them to pray and to have a love for the scriptures. Teach them to observe the Sabbath Day, to keep it holy. These basics will lay a proper foundation for additional teachings.

WHEN TO TEACH. Parents must make an intentional effort to teach at home. L. Tom Perry wisely suggested some things parents can do to create stronger family cultures: "Parents can hold family prayer, scripture study, and family home evenings and eat together as often as possible, making dinner a time of communication and the teaching of values."[14] Linda S. Reeves echoes these sentiments as she declared, "Daily scripture study and prayer and weekly family home evening are the very practices that help take away stress, give direction to our lives, and add protection to our homes."[15] Clearly, these three crucial habits are vital times for teaching children.

Family Prayer. "Family prayer should be a nonnegotiable priority in your daily life," counseled Richard G. Scott. He continued, "Parents, help safeguard your children by arming them morning and night with the power of family prayer. Children are bombarded every day with sinful behaviors. Protect your children from daily worldly influences by fortifying them with the powerful blessings that result from family prayer."[16] President Spencer W. Kimball cautioned: "In the past, having family prayer once a day may have been all right. But in the future, it will not be enough if we are going to save our families."[17]

These are some sobering thoughts that deserve careful consideration. Some parents may get discouraged trying to hold family prayer because of conflicting work and school schedules, which make it seem impossible to gather their families to the same place at the same time. A creative solution to this dilemma may be to have more than one family prayer each morning and evening.

Remember, it is through family prayer that children become acquainted with many eternal family values. It not only teaches love for God but confirms that He is there. The end result is worth whatever sacrifices we make to build the habit—and often these are no more than small sacrifices of time. President Gordon B. Hinckley shared, "I know of no single practice that will have a more salutary effect upon your lives than the practice of kneeling together as you begin and close each day. There is no substitute for family prayer."[18]

Scripture Study. We talk to God through prayer. He most often communicates back to us through His written word in the scriptures and the words of the living prophets. If you want your children to recognize, understand, and act on the promptings of the Spirit, you must study the scriptures with them. Methods for family scripture study do not matter. What matters is that it is consistent and that it is daily.

Many prophetic blessings are promised to those who dedicate time to daily studying the scriptures. One blessing is that peace will prevail in our homes—not that challenges will cease—but that we will find peace in the turmoil around us. We will be wise to follow Richard G. Scott's counsel: "Feasting on the word of God each day is more important than sleep, school, work, television shows, video games, or social media. You may need to reorganize your priorities to provide time for the study of the word of God. If so, do it!"[19]

Family Home Evening. What makes family home evening successful? The success of family home evening is simply in making sure that you have it. Be cautious not to make your family home evening just an afterthought of a busy day. Decide that on Monday night (or another night that works best) your family will be together at home for the evening.

The structure of your evening is not as important as the time invested. Make it a meaningful experience for each member of the family. Here is one example of how family home evening could look:

* Start and end with prayer. This invites the Spirit, increases love, and teaches your family how to pray.
* Learn from the scriptures and the words of latter-day prophets to help your family live the gospel.
* Add music, such as hymns and Primary songs, to create an atmosphere of love, peace, and joy.
* Make it fun by playing games, acting out scripture stories, and making treats. Keep the atmosphere light and loving
* Be consistent.

In the words of Elder Richard G. Scott: "Family home evening is a precious time to bear testimony in a safe environment; to learn teaching, planning, and organizational skills; to strengthen family bonds; to develop family traditions; to talk to each other; and more important, to have a marvelous time together!"[20]

Eat Together. Mealtime traditionally has been the time when all the members of the family come together. It is one of the most important moments in family time. But for meals to be positive, they need to be a time when we are focusing on building relationships more than we are focusing on good nutrition or keeping elbows off the table. We can use that mealtime to be a time to talk about what was good during the day, anything fun or interesting that happened, or for parents to volunteer things about their day rather than just ask children, "What did you do today?"

Increasingly, families don't spend very many meals together. "This is most concerning," observed President Dallin H. Oaks, "because the time a family spends together eating meals at home is the strongest predictor of children's academic achievement and psychological adjustment." He continued, "Family mealtimes have also been shown to be a strong bulwark against children's smoking, drinking, or using drugs. There is inspired wisdom in this advice to parents: what your children really want for dinner is you."[21]

HOW TO TEACH. You are always teaching, even when you are not aware of it. As parents, we teach children what we already are, more by attitude and example than by words. For example, if parents are honest with their children, children learn honesty. If parents listen and care about their children, then children learn to listen and care. Children learn to value what we actually value, not what we tell them to value—not what we *say* we value, but what we actually value. Children will notice whether you treat the scriptures respectfully. They will observe how you speak about Heavenly Father and Jesus Christ. They will watch how you live the principles you are teaching. Actions speak louder than words. Your righteous example will help them develop greater feelings of love and respect for Heavenly Father and His Son.

Though it is our actions that speak most distinctly to our children, our words are of great importance. How unfortunate it is when children do not hear their parents tell them often of their love for Heavenly Father. When a parent speaks words of faith to a child, his love for his heavenly parents grows. Elder Loren C. Dunn emphasized:

> Parents should bear their testimonies to their children in
> the home—actually express to your children exactly what

it is about the Church you know to be true. If we think our children know these things just because they live in the same house with us, we are mistaken. We need to say the words so our families can feel the same spirit of testimony that we have felt. Family home evening is an ideal time for this to take place.[22]

The idea that God exists comes by testimony. Human testimony is always accompanied by the Spirit. It is the basis of faith. Bear testimony to your children.

After setting a good example for children and bearing testimony to them, a final principle for effective teaching is summarized by Elder Neal A. Maxwell in these words: "Do not be afraid of repetitious teaching."[23] President Ezra Taft Benson also taught: "Sound principles and eternal truths need to be frequently repeated so that we do not forget their application nor become dissuaded by other arguments."[24] In other words, one family home evening lesson on faith is not enough to ensure that your children will learn that principle. So it is with all the principles and doctrines that you teach. There is great truth in the Latin proverb which says, "Repetition is the mother of learning." According to Elder David A. Bednar, "Repetition is a vehicle through which the Holy Ghost can enlighten our minds, influence our hearts, and enlarge our understanding."[25]

> "**R**epetition is the mother of learning."

PERSONAL INVITATION. Take a moment to reflect upon the teaching opportunities in your home. Is there a need for improvement? Consider Elder Bednar's words: "Each family prayer, each episode of family scripture study, and each family home evening is a brushstroke on the canvas of our souls. No one event may appear to be very impressive or memorable. But…our consistency in doing seemingly small things can lead to significant spiritual results."[26]

Parenting is expensive—not only in money—but also in time and effort. It is the most expensive activity in the world, but it is also the most rewarding and important activity in the world. Perhaps you have made many mistakes. Perhaps for years you have done the wrong things. But the very next breath or step you take, the very next word you say can be in a new direction than the one you have been taking.

WEEKLY ASSIGNMENT

Our puzzle piece this week will include two additional and crucial internal evaluations. The first is to evaluate your children's work. Do your children know what jobs are expected of them and how to properly do them? Is their work organized in a manner to motivate them in fun ways? Do they feel your love and appreciation when they complete their tasks? Secondly, consider the level of teaching that currently exists in your home. Make plans to enhance teaching moments and be more deliberate in your teaching methods.

GUIDING PRINCIPLES AND PRACTICES

Principle #9: Through punishment a parent controls a child's actions; through good discipline a parent teaches a child to control his own actions.

Principle #10: Work is a blessing and not only promotes happiness but teaches responsibility.

Practice #9: Use discipline rather than punishment with children.
Practice #10: Organize children's work.

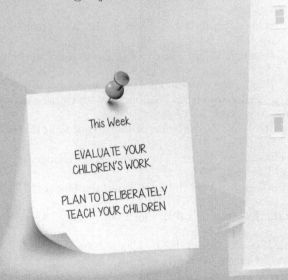

This Week

EVALUATE YOUR
CHILDREN'S WORK

PLAN TO DELIBERATELY
TEACH YOUR CHILDREN

Notes

1. Gottman, *Raising an Emotionally Intelligent Child*, 19.
2. Ibid., 23-24.
3. Daryl V. Hoole, *The Art of Teaching Children*, (Salt Lake City: Deseret Book, 1975), 229.
4. Gene R. Cook, *Raising Up a Family to the Lord*, (Salt Lake City: Deseret Book, 1993), 179.
5. Quoted by Elwood R. Peterson, *Ensign*, June 1972, 9.
6. Neal A. Maxwell, "Gospel of Work," *Friend*, June 1975, 7.
7. Neal A. Maxwell, "The Man of Christ," *Ensign*, May 1975, 101.
8. Joe J. Christensen, "Greed, Selfishness, and Overindulgence," *Ensign*, May 1999, 9-10.
9. Hoole, *The Art of Teaching Children*, 223-236.
10. Eyre, *Teaching Children Responsibility*, 55-56.
11. Ibid., 58-59.
12. Gordon B. Hinckley, "Bring Up a Child in the Way He Should Go," *Ensign*, Nov. 1993, 59-60.
13. Faust, "The Greatest Challenge in the World—Good Parenting," 33.
14. L. Tom Perry, "Becoming Goodly Parents," *Ensign*, Nov. 2012, 28.
15. Linda S. Reeves, "Protection from Pornography—a Christ-Focused Home," *Ensign*, May 2014, 16-17.
16. Richard G. Scott, "Make the Exercise of Faith Your First Priority," *Ensign*. Nov. 2014, 93.
17. Spencer W. Kimball, in Faust, The Greatest Challenge in the World—Good Parenting," 33.
18. Gordon B. Hinckley, "Except the Lord Build the House," *Ensign*, June 1971, 72.
19. Scott, "Make the Exercise of Faith Your First Priority," 93.
20. Ibid., 94.
21. Dallin H. Oaks, "Good, Better, Best," *Ensign*, Nov. 2007, 106.
22. Loren C. Dunn, "How to Gain a Testimony," *Ensign*, Jan. 1973, 85.
23. Neal A. Maxwell, in David A. Bednar, *Act in Doctrine*, (Salt Lake City: Deseret Book, 2012), 124.

24. Ezra Taft Benson, "The Honored Place of Woman," *Ensign*, Nov. 1981, 104-105.
25. David A. Bednar, "Repeat Over Again...the Same Things as Before," BYU—Idaho Devotional address, Jan. 26, 2016.
26. David A. Bednar, "More Diligent and Concerned at Home," *Ensign*, Nov. 2009, 19-20.

Chapter 7
Overcoming Anger/ Resolving Conflict

Successful families don't just happen. It takes every bit of combined energy, talent, desire, vision, and determination you can muster to build the family culture you have envisioned. Keep in mind that when you're working with your family, "slow" is "fast" and "fast" is "slow." This is simply another way of saying, "Be patient. Go slowly." Acknowledge the miracle of the Chinese bamboo tree, and do not get discouraged if your initial efforts meet with resistance. Just smile and keep moving forward. My promise to you is that it will be worth the effort.

The metaphor of the airplane reminds us that our destination is within reach and that the journey can be rich, enriching, and joyful. In fact, the journey is really part of the destination, because in the family, as in life, how you travel is as important as where you arrive.

Proclamation-Based

EVALUATION OF CHILDREN'S WORK AND DELIBERATE TEACHING PLAN ASSIGNMENT

Do you feel good about the way your children's work is organized? What about the teaching moments in your home? Are they happening consistently and deliberately? Teaching children to work and having a deliberate plan for teaching in our family are two critical elements of the teaching layer of the pyramid.

Let me share three of my favorite teaching quotes:

♦ Elder L. Tom Perry: "We can organize our families based on clear, simple family rules and expectations, wholesome family traditions and rituals, and 'family economics,' where children have household responsibilities and can earn allowances so that they can learn to budget, save, and pay tithing on the money they earn."[1]

♦ Elder Quentin L. Cook: "Parents, the days are long past when regular, active participation in Church meetings and programs, though essential, can fulfill your sacred responsibility to teach your children to live moral, righteous lives and walk uprightly before the Lord...Spiritual maturity must flourish in our homes."[2]

♦ Elder Kevin W. Pearson: "We can give our children education, lessons, athletics, the arts, and material possessions, but if we do not give them faith in Christ, we have given little."[3]

Consider two insightful principles taught by Elder Lynn G. Robbins: 1) "Effective teaching is the very essence of parenting." 2) "The most important work you will ever do is to effectively teach your children."[4]

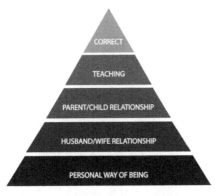

CORRECTION

With six pieces of the parenting puzzle in place we are at last ready to discuss the top layer of the pyramid—the one most parents want to begin with—correction. How do we handle misbehavior in our children? Loving our children unconditionally does not mean we say and do nothing when they make mistakes. Children do need to be corrected, but they do not need the disappointment and anger we almost always administer along with the instruction we offer. The moment we are irritated, our children correctly sense that we don't love them unconditionally, and the effect is always disastrous.

Although we're mostly unaware of it, we use our disappointment and anger to control our children's behavior. They will often do what we want in order to avoid our expression of those terrible feelings, but that eliminates the possibility of their feeling unconditional love from us. Being permissive with children, however, is as destructive as controlling them. What children need is correction that is given with genuine acceptance.

CHILDREN COMMUNICATE WITH BEHAVIOR

"Do you love me?" Most behavior in children is determined by how much he or she feels loved. If their emotional tank is full, you will see it in their behavior. If their emotional tank is empty, you will see it in their behavior. The primary cause of misbehavior in children is an empty emotional tank. It is not fair or wise on the part of a parent to demand good behavior from a child without first filling his emotional tank.[5]

> *The primary cause of misbehavior in children is an empty emotional tank.*

HANDLING MISBEHAVIOR. When a child misbehaves, we usually ask, "What can I do to correct his behavior?" This approach usually leads to punishment. A child will not feel loved if his misbehavior is handled in this way. What we should ask when a child misbehaves is, "What does this child need?" Is there a physical problem? (He could be hungry, sick, or tired.) Is the misbehavior related to a developmental stage? (Perhaps he is a two-year-old.) Does the child lack knowledge of the situation, or does he have an empty tank? This doesn't mean that misbehavior is condoned. Misbehavior should not be condoned, but we must take care of the cause as well as the misbehavior. It is better to give a child what he needs—eye contact, physical contact, focused attention, water, food, or a nap—instead of punishment.[6]

Yelling. Often yelling is used for handling misbehavior. Yelling at children to get them to do something is like using the horn to stop a car from going downhill. It makes a lot of noise without good results.

Spanking. The practice of spanking was common when I was a child. It was also an option I tried when I was a young, inexperienced mom. Much controversy exists debating the effectiveness of this practice. The biggest problem with spanking is that it is done for the wrong reasons. Spanking is a sign of bankruptcy on the part of parents; they are out of ideas, feel desperate and are frustrated. Spanking is used for the release of parents' emotions instead of as a means for the discipline and training of children.

Time-Out. As an alternative to spanking, another negative consequence for behavior problems in children has become popular. Time-out involves temporarily sending a misbehaving child to a designated place until they are "ready" to return. On the surface, time-outs seem sensible. They are non-violent but still get the child's attention. Plus, they give the parent and child a much-needed break from each other while emotions run high. Do you use time-out? Do you like it? Does it work?

Quite frankly, I have a problem with time-out. What message does it send? Quite literally, the message is, "Go to your room!" Early childhood experts point out that time-out must be used with care due to its potentially negative side effects. Particularly in the case of young children, time-out can be considered:

- an imposed external control of behavior that takes away a child's opportunity to build his own internal controls
- a way to meet the adult's need to maintain order without addressing the child's needs in a constructive way
- a negative experience that can affect the child's developing

> sense of self-worth and self-confidence, particularly if done in front of family members and peers
- a missed opportunity for valuable learning experiences that are forfeited during these periods of isolation

For these reasons, a parent should carefully balance the benefits of using time-out against the potential negative effects. Although time-out may be perfectly appropriate in some situations, experts recommend that in most situations, time-out should not be the default choice for handling children's misbehavior.[7]

SO, WHAT DO WE DO INSTEAD? Instead of yelling. Instead of spanking. Instead of using time-out. Instead of grounding, denying privileges, criticizing, blaming, and a host of other negative consequences employed by the "natural parent." What we do instead is to use the parenting style we discussed in Chapter 1.

THE AUTHORITATIVE PARENTING STYLE

We recall that this approach to parenting is most consistent with the scriptures and teachings from Church leaders. Authoritative parents combine the motivating power of warmth and affection with guidance and control to promote positive outcomes in children.[8] This is **proclamation-based** parenting.

When children act in ways that are inappropriate, rather than simply reacting to the behavior, authoritative parents implement positive regulation solutions which have been carefully thought out in advance. Let's consider an analogy that might clarify how to choose an appropriate regulation strategy.

THE SITUATION. Suppose for a minute that you show up late for work several mornings in a row.

Scenario A. Your boss storms into your office and in front of your colleagues yells, "This is the third time in a row that you have come in late. I am sick and tired of having to deal with this kind of behavior. Either you get your act together, or you are out of here!"

Scenario B. Your boss calls you into his office. He indicates that he has noticed that you have been coming to work late for the last several days. "Is there something wrong?" he inquires. You explain your reasons, which include a family situation that has created some stress. He is flexible and indicates that he would prefer that you get to work on time, but until the family situation gets under control, he would be willing to have you make up the time missed by staying later on some days. He reiterates his confidence in you as an employee and expresses his appreciation for the contribution you make to the company.

Which of the two bosses would you rather have?

PARENTING APPLICATION. Think more closely about how this applies to parenting regulation strategies.

Boss A humiliated the employee in front of others; Boss B spoke in private. Children deserve the same respect, with regulation being carried out in private settings when possible.

Boss A raised his voice; Boss B calmly discussed the situation. Children deserve to not be yelled at.

Boss A threatened the employee; Boss B tried to find out what was wrong. While helping children to see the consequences of their actions is the parents' responsibility, threatening children is an ineffective parenting practice, particularly when done in anger.

Boss A did not ask and did not seem to care about the employee's point of view; Boss B was willing to negotiate a solution that worked for everyone. Authoritative parents take time to listen and negotiate a solution to fill the needs of all involved.

MORAL TO THE STORY. Children need to be treated with respect even when they have done something wrong—just like you would wish to be treated with respect by your employer. Finally, compare the degree of loyalty to the company and the employee's likelihood of improving the late-coming behavior when working under Boss A or Boss B. If children are treated with respect, like the

115

employee with Boss B, they will be more motivated to correct their behavior and will develop a stronger sense of loyalty to their parents.

THE THREE "BE'S"

In just a few words, we can summarize some regulation strategy guidelines for authoritative parents as follows:

BE CLEAR. Children need structure and direction. Limits give children a sense of security, provide order, prevent injuries and problems, and help family members work cooperatively and harmoniously with one another.

Establish Family Rules. Stated positively and few in number, rules should be easily understood by all family members.

Provide friendly reminders. Children will have moments when they really do not feel motivated or are not interested in complying with parental requests. It's hard to be good all of the time. Restate the expectation as a friendly reminder to give the child a second chance.

Use reasoning. Positive explanations help children understand the whys and hows of a particular rule or expectation. For example, a parent might explain to a child who is just learning to ride a bike: "I know that it's exciting to be able to ride fast and far, but right now your boundaries are this mailbox to that corner. When you get older, we will let you ride farther by yourself, but for now, it's important that you ride your bike close to our house so we can help you if you fall and we can make sure that you hear any cars coming up behind you so you can steer closer to the sidewalk."

Teach appropriate behavior. Consider yourself a coach to your children. When a player needs to improve his playing, his coach explains specific changes that he needs to make to achieve better performance. In a similar way, parents can coach their children to help them improve, whether it be cleaning a toilet or not speaking in a whining voice.

BE POSITIVE. How we respond and act affects our children. Therefore, as parents, we want to be able to guide and shape our children in the most positive ways possible.

Emphasize the dos rather than the don'ts. "Quit running in the house!" "Stop hitting!" "Don't touch that vase!" "Don't stay on the phone so long!" Although such statements may stop undesirable behavior in the short term, they do nothing in terms of teaching a child about what they *can* do, and they often create negative feelings. A positive approach turns these statements around, providing clear direction. For example, "Remember, run outside." "Remember to use your words instead of your fists." "You can look at the vase but remember that it might fall and break if you touch it." "Please keep your call to twenty minutes because I need your help with dinner." Emphasizing the dos sets a better climate in the home.

Avoid saying, "No." Kids barrage us with questions every day. Often, our answer is "no." Find opportunities to say "yes" when you can. If your daughter asks to go to the indoor pool in the middle of a busy weekday, try saying, "Going to the pool sounds like so much fun. Should we go tomorrow after school or on Saturday?" Be prepared to say "yes" or to redirect them to a more positive option.

Use positive reinforcement. Children respond enthusiastically to positive reinforcement. Good behavior in children can be motivated by sincere praise, token rewards, or special privileges.

Use requests instead of commands. It is important to maintain pleasantness with children. "Would you please bring me that book?" is a pleasant request. "Bring me that book," is a less pleasant command. Commands may be needed *occasionally* when a child does not carry out a request. If you normally use pleasant requests, occasional commands are quite effective, especially when a rapid response is needed.

Use humor. Humor can relieve the stress of the moment, turn a potentially negative situation into a positive one, and ultimately enhance the connection you feel with your children. Appropriate humor does not create laughter at the expense of a child's feelings; rather, it makes the circumstance fun and alleviates family tension.

Tone of voice. We communicate much more with our tone and our body language than we do with the words we use. The younger your child is, the more he will listen to everything but your words. Be aware of the tone of voice you use when speaking to your children and make adjustments if necessary. Keep it positive!

BE FIRM. Prophets and the scriptures tell us that love and firmness should always go together. Exercising firmness without love is harshness. Trying to be loving without being firm is indulgence. Being firm doesn't mean being unpleasant, and loving firmness doesn't require anger or loudness. We must be firm, but we'll be just as effective by doing it pleasantly.

Set limits. Love and affection do not foster permissiveness; lack of firmness and limit-setting does. Setting limits to a child is like a fence to a cow. Just as the cow noses her way along the fence to feel that it is there, children have the natural urge to find the fence. They want to know it's there. This gives them confidence and a feeling of security and protection. However, we must not fence the child in too much or this might force him to jump the fence. Endeavor instead to build the right kind of fence for him to feel free to do what he should do within its bounds.

Use effective consequences. What makes a consequence effective? We must be careful how we impose consequences. If we apply them with anger, they become punishments, which rarely benefit anyone. Punishment only heightens the fear and anger of the person being punished. He is then *more* likely—not less—to require future punishment, and when that happens, we haven't helped anyone.

Consequences should always be something besides adult anger, lectures, or rejection. Appropriate consequences include situations that temporarily prevent the misbehavior. A consequence may be simply your talking to children about their behavior or breaking a rule, so they know you are serious about the rules. Consistency is important. If you sometimes scold a child for leaving toys out, yet sometimes pick them up, the child has no way of learning the importance of cleaning up.

Use natural consequences when possible. For example, if a child breaks something, he must replace it; if a child uses a marker on the wall, he must scrub the wall. Natural consequences are not always as easy as scolding, but they are much more effective.

A critical principle to understand about consequences is that consequences should always be logically connected to the child's actions. The connection between arguing with a sibling and being kept home from a school activity is probably not clear to most children. When a consequence is not clearly connected to the transgression, it is punishing rather than teaching.

Consequences can only be effectively administered by a parent who feels love for the child. Parents can sometimes impose consequences that are so harsh that the punishing intent is obvious.[9] Often, consequences are delivered with a coldness that promotes a sense of isolation and desperation in the child. This is not how Heavenly Father delivers consequences to us.

The key to effective consequences: If you feel bad later, you acted as a natural parent and did it wrong! Now what? Take heart and keep reading for the answer.

THE FOURTH "BE"

Be: Clear
Positive
Firm
Consistently Inconsistent

119

President James E. Faust taught: "Child rearing is so individualistic. Every child is different and unique. What works with one may not work with another. I do not know who is wise enough to say what discipline is too harsh or what is too lenient except the parents of the children themselves, who love them most. It is a matter of prayerful discernment for the parents. Certainly the overarching and undergirding principle is that the discipline of children must be motivated more by love than by punishment."[10]

This inspired counsel teaches us that we must be *consistent* in our unconditional love for each child yet *inconsistent* in the way each situation is handled—according to the needs of the child. This is the example that Christ set for us as he ministered to people. He healed the blind in different ways: anointing the eyes with a clay made of spittle to be washed away, merely touching the eyes, spitting on the eyes and laying hands on them, simply speaking the word of healing.[11] Likewise, he ministered to the adulterous woman—not according to the letter of the law—but in a manner that showed love even though he did not condone adultery.[12] Christ was inconsistent in his methods because He knew each person and treated them individually in the way they needed to learn. He focused on what helped people rather than emphasizing punishment for wrongdoing.

The most important thing to remember as we correct our children is that our actions must not shut off the Spirit. This being said, and knowing that parents are imperfect people who will make frequent mistakes, what should you do after you have made a poor choice in imposing a consequence or have expressed anger to a child? Apologize and ask for forgiveness. If a parent can sincerely say, "I'm sorry," that doesn't in any way lessen their authority or power in the home. It actually invites the child to see them in a different light. When a parent can say to a child, "I'm sorry. I've disappointed you. I was wrong. Forgive me," I think that is perhaps stronger than "I love you."

ANGER: PARENTS' WORST ENEMY IN RAISING CHILDREN

Let's discuss anger. Anger draws nothing but disrespect. It is called another of the "deadly sins" by Neal A. Maxwell. *Anger is the destroyer of family relations.* Lynn G. Robbins described anger as the "thought-sin that leads to hostile feelings or behavior. It is the detonator of road rage on the freeway, flare-ups in the sports arena, and domestic violence in homes."[13] Expressions of anger and resentment occur too frequently in families. Some parents think contention is part of child rearing. Irritations and frustrations will occur, but frequent anger and contention do not persist where the gospel of Jesus Christ is practiced.

ANGER IS A CODE. Anger is not usually the primary, or first, emotion. We convert primary feelings into anger. Consider the following examples:

Fear. Imagine that you are shopping with your four-year-old son in tow when suddenly you find him missing. Frantically, you search the crowds as a cold lump of fear wells up inside. Then, you spot him sitting behind a counter, nonchalantly playing with some papers. Jerking him up, you angrily scold him for not staying by your side. Although you are angry now, your first feeling was *fear*.

Frustration. You are in a hurry to straighten the garage before visiting relatives arrive. As fast as you put one thing away, your six-year-old drags out something else. With frustration mounting, you suddenly yell at him to leave. Your initial *frustration* turned to anger and the raising of your voice.

Fatigue. Exhausted after a long day at work, you open the door at home and are greeted by two sons loudly requesting allowance increases. You bark a hasty reply. *Fatigue* was quickly translated into hostility.

Embarrassment and humiliation. Your son acts up in front of company and your embarrassment grows. Finally, you snap and angrily send him to his room. He responds by calling you a name. *Embarrassment* became anger, and *humiliation* turned into fury.

Repeatedly, we convert primary feelings—worry, guilt, disappointment, rejection, injustice, shock, uncertainty, confusion—into anger. Knowing that anger covers a prior emotion helps you to deal with it more effectively, both in yourself and in your children.

Seeing anger as a code makes it less threatening.[14]

BREAKING THE CODE. A concerned mother once asked a family therapist, "How do I get my son to stop being angry and rebellious all the time?" The therapist wisely replied, "Maybe you need to find out *why* he's angry before you try to *control* his anger. If a fire alarm goes off in a building, is it wise to simply turn it off, or should someone try to find out what triggered the alarm?"[15]

This is what we mean by breaking the anger code. We accept a child's anger by using emotion coaching to put their feelings into words as this dad demonstrated when his daughter, Carolyn, called him a name:

Dad: Carolyn, you're terribly upset with me.

Carolyn: I sure am! How come I have to go to bed at eight and Jimmy gets to stay up till nine? He gets all the privileges around here—just because he's older. I can't help it that I got born too late!

Dad: It feels awfully unfair not getting the same privileges, and kinda like there's no way to get ahead of him.

Carolyn: Yeah, it sure does.

Dad: And it makes you mad that Mom and I allow this kind of thing.

Carolyn: You can say that again. It's all because of you that I got born second anyway. 'Course, I guess if you have more than one kid, someone has to be second, but I don't like being the youngest.

Dad: There are just too many disadvantages to being youngest.

Carolyn: Right! (*more quietly*) Of course, sometimes I like it cuz I don't have to do as many chores as Jimmy does.

Dad: Sometimes you see advantages to being second.

Carolyn: (*smiling gently*) Yeah, guess I like all the advantages and none of the disadvantages.

When we accept anger in children by helping them to name their feelings, the code is cracked. Steam is released and real feelings surface. Carolyn tells her dad that her hostility comes from feeling shortchanged.[16] What would have happened if Dad would have reacted negatively to the name-calling and punished Carolyn?

ANGER IS A CHOICE. It is a fact of life that anger is one of our many emotions. A popular view of this fact is that we are not responsible for our feelings. Others *cause* us to be angry. Our only choice is *how* we show anger. This is not true. Anger is a choice we make. Emotions are responses to a stimulus, and a stimulus has no emotional charge. Emotion comes from within because of how we choose to see a stimulus. If you doubt this, consider the response you would have to having grape juice spilled on your brand-new carpet, either by your five-year-old or by a dear friend visiting from out of state!

EXPRESSION OF ANGER. Anger is typically expressed in three ways—two of the ways being destructive.

Directed outward. When we express anger outwardly, we do so in aggressive ways: screaming, punching someone, smashing something, throwing a book across the room. Aggressive expressions of anger usually make the problem worse. Studies have shown that "venting anger" through physical aggression, such as punching a bag or a pillow, actually increased aggressive behavior.[17]

Directed inward. Suppressing angry feelings by holding them inside without allowing some form of constructive expression is destructive to a person's health. Certain health risks are increased including high blood pressure, depression, suicide, gastrointestinal problems, and drug or alcohol use. Also, chances of passive-aggressive behavior and hostility toward others is increased.[18]

Control of anger. Popular psychology once recommended that people should freely communicate their anger. Research has shown that this makes matters worse. It is wise to control or manage anger in constructive ways. Controlling anger does not mean ignoring the emotion. Instead, it involves first calming yourself so that you can use the emotion constructively.

Think of anger as a wild horse. Few people would be willing to ride a wild horse without a bridle. The purpose of a bridle is to get the horse to do what we want it to do. Using a bridle doesn't deny that the horse exists, nor does it mean that the horse is a bad animal. A bridle allows us to manage and guide the horse to accomplish our purposes. Anger is like an unbridled horse. Unless we govern it, we

123

are at its mercy.

A VALUABLE LIFE LESSON. *Handling* anger in a child is perhaps the most difficult part of parenting. Because it is difficult, most parents respond to a child's anger in wrong and destructive ways. *Teaching* a child how to handle anger is one of the most important responsibilities in parenting and one of the most difficult for two reasons: 1) It doesn't come naturally—our natural response is becoming more angry; 2) It is a long and tedious process—no child can be expected to learn to handle anger quickly.

Anger is not something to be "disciplined" out of a child. One of life's most valuable lessons is to teach children by words and actions that choosing *not* to respond in anger *is* within our control. If we throw or bang things, hit, scream, yell, or swear—our children are likely to follow our example. More children are punished for mimicking their parents than for disobeying their parents. On the other hand, our example of love, helpfulness, tolerance, and cooperation can set a pattern for children to follow in handling their angry feelings.

ANGER IS ROOTED IN SELFISHNESS. Anger is always selfish and makes happiness impossible. Persons responding with anger are saying that their feelings and opinions are more important than the feelings and opinions of others. Selfish people use anger to control others and to manipulate children. When they raise their voice and act mad, it makes others give in to them. Children adopt anger as a way to respond to anything that they can't control. A pattern of anger is established and passed from parents to children—generation to generation—till the cycle is broken.

NEGATIVE FEELINGS. All negative feelings can turn to anger. The unmet needs of an infant will culminate in an angry cry. The life of a preschooler holds thousands of frustrations, which if not eliminated, will produce angry outbursts.[19]

Tantrums. Young children usually let you know directly when they are angry. A tantrum is nothing more than intense communications shrieking: "I've lost control!" "I'm extremely frustrated!" Here is a helpful list of some "dos and don'ts" in dealing with tantrums in children:

1) DON'T take it personally. Young children have not yet learned to control anger.

2) DON'T heap your anger upon theirs. Children have no defense against parental anger. This closes off all normal ways for the child to express anger.

3) DON'T suppress their anger. This is one of the most destructive things we can force a young child to do. It leads to passive-aggressive behavior.

4) DON'T isolate an angry child. Sending a child away creates a sense of rejection and more negative feelings. Our goal is to reduce emotional burdens, not to increase them.

1) DO understand child development. Realize that children learn to handle anger gradually as they develop through the stages. A child cannot be expected to handle anger maturely until age six or seven.

2) DO distract a child before anger reaches its peak. Tantrums usually build up gradually. Interrupt it before it happens by redirecting a child's attention—nip it in the bud.

3) DO stay with a child during anger. It may be unpleasant for you, but this is part of helping him deal with his feelings.

4) DO show an increase of love to the child once he calms down. Hugs and comforting words will restore the relationship and strengthen the child's sense of security.

Paul's story. Four-year-old Paul's parents are unaware that tantrums disguise lost controls. They see "bratty" behavior; consequently, they spank. What are the results of this treatment?

Put yourself in Paul's shoes for a moment. First, he is totally and completely frustrated by some situation he cannot handle. (At four his controls are poorly developed.) At the precise moment when he is overloaded with emotions he can't get on top of, he receives a resounding slap. Now he has a whole new set of feelings to deal with: *hurt* from the slap; *frustration* at not being understood; *resentment* that his parents don't help; *helplessness* to retaliate directly; and *fear* of further punishment. The result: more negative feelings than ever.

"But," counters his father, "when I slap, he stops the tantrum—and right away!" Sure, the *symptom* stops, but why? It stops out of fear. On the surface, the slap looks effective. But what happens to all the feelings that caused the tantrum? And what does Paul do with all the new feelings generated by the slap? He may repress them, but eventually they will come out in any of the countless ways that hidden feelings make their presence known. The lesson Paul learns is that it is better to repress his feelings than to express them.

How would you feel if, when you were absolutely beside yourself, the most important person in your life hit you? We must see a tantrum for what it truly is: a communication of extreme frustration.[20]

OVERCOMING ANGER. Since anger is rooted in selfishness, the way to overcome anger is to overcome selfishness. What we need is empathy and compassion in our relationships. The following story is a perfect illustration of what is possible when we become empathetic and compassionate with our children. I call it "The Story of the Vacuum Cleaner."

Ann had just finished straightening the living room in preparation for guests who would arrive in an hour. As she walked back into the room, she couldn't believe what she saw.

Right in the middle of her perfectly cleaned room, four-year-old Elizabeth had dumped the contents of the vacuum, spreading a filthy dust pile nearly three feet wide in front of the fireplace. She was looking up at her mother with a helpless expression.

"What are you doing?" were the first, almost automatic words that escaped from Ann's lips.

"I don't know!" cried the frustrated child, knowing that her mother had reason to be angry.

Her words suddenly made Ann see the situation from her daughter's perspective. Her anger vanished as she realized that Elizabeth had watched her preparing the room for guests and had known that vacuuming the room was a usual part of her mother's preparations. So, she had attempted to help. Somehow, though, as she dragged the vacuum into the room, the bag had come loose on the floor.

When Ann saw the situation from her daughter's point of view, her initial feelings of anger melted into understanding. Without pretense, Ann was able to scoop Elizabeth up in her arms and say, "Thank you for helping me with this big job. I appreciate you very, very much. Can you help me put that dirt back in the vacuum so we can finish this job together?"

Recalling the incident, Ann says, "As upset as I was, I was able to see through my false desire to control Elizabeth and recognize that she had been trying to help me. That recognition softened my heart, and I responded the way I would like to always."[21]

No amount of anger would have cleaned the mess up any sooner, nor would Elizabeth have learned through a demonstration of anger any worthwhile lesson that would prevent future accidents. But if Ann had responded in anger, what Elizabeth *would* have learned was that anger is the appropriate response in this situation.

Kids do what they do for reasons that make perfect sense to them. Understanding is the key. When we see situations from their point of view, we will seldom lose our temper as we are trying to understand. On the other hand, when we "flood" (overreact to) kids, we overwhelm them, and they don't hear anything we say. The only thing they will remember is our angry face.

Dealing with anger in ourselves. To handle anger in yourself, you must first accept this feeling and see it for what it is: a code signaling the presence of an earlier emotion. Catch hold of the *first* feeling and share *it* rather than the code. Anger frightens children; sharing primary emotions reduces fear.

Remember that anger is a choice. What we need is a "pause button"—something that enables us to stop between what happens to us and our response to it—and to choose our own response. Develop a coping strategy to use during that pause: count to ten, breathe deeply, take a walk, leave the room, get a drink of water, bite your tongue. Giving yourself even a few extra seconds before reacting can make a difference. Pressing the pause button gives you a chance to rewind, make a good choice, and then press play again to continue in a better way. One of this week's assignments will be to use a pause button on your anger.

The solution to anger is spiritual. Nephite prophets recorded: "There was no contention in the land because of the love of God which did dwell in the hearts of the people" (4 Nephi 1:15). When we are motivated by love and not selfishness, anger will not influence our relationships.

Pray with real intent for help in overcoming angry feelings. Specifically, our prayers can include asking that we will have the right kinds of feelings about others, that we will be able to control our negative feelings, that we will see others the way the Savior sees them—the gift of charity. Charity is the long-term answer to overcoming anger.

President Joseph F. Smith emphasized the importance of being kind to children instead of being angry: "When you speak or talk to them, do it not in anger, do it not harshly, in a condemning spirit. Speak to them kindly;. . .weep with them if necessary. . .The man that will be angry at his boy, and try to correct him while he is in anger, is in the greatest fault. . .You can only correct your children by love, in kindness, by love unfeigned, by persuasion, and reason."[22]

RESOLVING CONFLICT

It is normal to have conflict. You can't raise children without conflict. The causes of conflict are many. Some parents are overly permissive, giving in to their children's whims until their children's behavior is out of control. Others are too restrictive, provoking their children to rebel. Some parents overreact to their children's normal drive for independence. Some children go astray and willfully engage in behavior that violates family rules and standards.

Resolving conflict is a part of the **proclamation-based** parenting process. The challenging thing for a parent is to figure out a way to resolve the conflict without destroying the relationship. Here are some helpful principles to assist in the quest for resolving conflict in our families.

LISTEN TO UNDERSTAND. As one of the elements in a "Come

Unto Me" relationship, when parents listen and seek to understand their upset, angry children, many conflicts are averted. Your child's angry feelings will often dissipate when he or she feels understood. You may also find that your own feelings and perspectives change.

REFUSE TO ARGUE. One of the basic principles for resolving conflict in the home is so simple that it is often overlooked. It involves living the higher law of Christ and refusing to argue. Quarreling and fighting cannot occur when one person refuses to engage in it. Christ is the perfect example. He was a continual victim, yet he did not strike back.

Some parents may think that a noncombative response gives children the upper hand, allows them to win arguments, and places them in control of family matters. This is not the case. Use the communication strategies of an authoritative parent and refuse to argue with your children. Refusing to argue will be another assignment for this week.

FOLLOW SCRIPTURAL GUIDELINES: When a child needs reproving, we can do so according to guidelines found in the scriptures: "Reproving betimes with sharpness, when moved upon by the Holy Ghost; and then showing forth afterwards an increase of love toward him whom thou hast reproved, lest he esteem thee to be his enemy" (Doctrine and Covenants 121:43).

Neal A. Maxwell taught that "betimes" means early or soon, suggesting that the reproof should occur soon after the incident so as to be understood.[23] Sharpness does not mean with anger or forcefulness, but clearly and distinctly. Never discipline when angry or out of control. Pause before acting. Then, show an increase of love after an intense session with a child, giving appropriate physical affection and focused attention.

SELECTIVELY ARBITRATE CONFLICTS: Children sometimes engage in arguments to get attention and to have the parents take their side. These arguments often place parents in a no-win position because they can never fully know how the conflict started and what has happened between the children. Often, the best help is given by taking a neutral position and by giving the children responsibility to solve the problem, as shown in the following example.

Sid and Vance. Dad entered the room as Sid, twelve, and Vance, nine, were wrestling on the floor, hitting and yelling at each other. Vance began to cry, and Sid called him a baby. Dad stepped in and pulled the boys apart.

Dad: What's going on between you two?

Sid: Vance started it.

Vance: I did not. You started it.

Dad: So, you're both blaming each other for starting the problem. *(Gives them responsibility for solving the problem.)* What do you think we should do to solve it?

Vance: Tell Sid to leave me alone.

Sid: Leave you alone? What about me? Who was it that took my cards and scattered them all over the floor? Leave my stuff alone, and we'll get along fine.

Dad: *(remains neutral)* So Vance, you're saying that Sid started it, and Sid, you're saying that Vance started it by taking your cards without asking.

Vance: Yeah, well who was it that took my CD without asking?

Dad: Both of you are blaming each other for taking things without asking. So, let me ask again, what needs to happen to solve this problem?

Sid: Tell Vance to grow up.

Vance: Why don't you grow up?

Dad: It sounds to me like you want to keep arguing. Maybe we ought to just stay here until you're ready to solve this.

Sid: I'm ready.

Vance: So am I.

Sid: Tell Vance he needs to ask before he borrows my things.

Vance: Sid never asks me before he takes my things. He needs to ask, too.

Dad: So, both of you want the other to ask before borrowing things. Is that right?

Sid: Yes.

Vance: I guess.

Dad: I like that suggestion. Is that agreeable to both of you?

Both boys: Yes.

What did Dad do to help the boys solve the problem? He was able to listen to both boys without taking sides. He remained neutral. Notice that he did not send them to their rooms until they were ready to solve it. One or both boys may have been delighted to be in their room, and the problem would not be settled. Instead, Dad remained with them until a solution was found.

Another important thing to keep in mind is that conflict between children may be a sign of an empty emotional tank or tanks. Part of the resolution may be taking steps to fill up the tanks.

TO SUMMARIZE

Parenting is difficult work. If we have a desire to improve our parenting skills, it would be wise to follow the principles exemplified by the one perfect parent. Our Father in Heaven has given us a perfect example of how we should parent through the ways He parents us. Heavenly Father is an authoritative parent:

- He gives us commandments, limits, and boundaries that are **clear**, as are His expectations of us.
- He provides us with the **positive** support necessary to meet those expectations through the loving gift of His "great plan of happiness" (Alma 42:8) as well as the sacrifice of His Son.
- When we fail to meet His expectations, He is **firm** in the consequences we face according to eternal laws.
- Yet, His unfailing and perfect love is **consistently** offered to us. He will not withdraw His constant love from us, although we may withdraw from Him at times.

We become more like Him as we learn to love as He loves. We love not as our children become more loveable, but as we are increasingly filled with His love. Ezra Taft Benson has reminded us that "above all else, children need to know and feel they are loved, wanted, and appreciated. They need to be assured of that often."[24] Times of correcting misbehavior offer some of our best opportunities to demonstrate concern, strengthen relationships, and show forth an increase of love.

WEEKLY ASSIGNMENT

Your seventh puzzle piece is two-fold. First, you will practice using a "pause button" whenever you feel anger. This means you will have to plan your coping strategy ahead of time and be ready to implement that strategy as soon as you press the button. Second, you will practice refusing to argue with your kids. This doesn't mean giving them the silent treatment during intense moments, rather you will respond in calm and positive ways, without becoming angry. Practice makes perfect!

GUIDING PRINCIPLES AND PRACTICES

Principle #11: Misbehavior in children must not be condoned.
Principle #12: Anger is the destroyer of family relations.
Practice #11: Use the authoritative parenting style.
Practice #12: Be an example to children by using an appropriate coping strategy to control anger.

This Week

USE A PAUSE BUTTON TO
CONTROL ANGER

REFUSE TO ARGUE

Notes
1. Perry, "Becoming Goodly Parents," 28.
2. Quentin L. Cook, "Can Ye Feel So Now?" *Ensign*, Nov. 2012, 8.
3. Kevin W. Pearson, "Faith in the Lord Jesus Christ," *Ensign*, May 2009, 38.
4. Lynn G. Robbins, *Love is a Choice*, (Salt Lake City: Deseret Book, 2015), 130.
5. Campbell, *How to Really Love Your Child*, 101.
6. Ibid., 102.
7. Mary Ellis Schreiber, "Time-outs for Toddlers: Is our goal punishment or education?" *Young Children*, July 1999, 22-25.
8. Laura E. Berk, *Awakening Children's Minds*, (New York: Oxford University Press, 2001), 50-51.
9. Scoresby, *In the Heart of a Child*, 71.
10. Faust, "The Greatest Challenge in the World—Good Parenting," 34.
11. See Matthew 9:27-30; 20:3-34; Mark 8:22-25; Luke 18:35-43.
12. See John 8:1-11.
13. Lynn G. Robbins, "Agency and Anger," *Ensign*, May 1998, 80-81.
14. Dorothy Corkille Briggs, *Your Child's Self-Esteem*, (Garden City: Doubleday & Company, 1970), 199-200.
15. Greg Baer, *Real Love*, (New York: Gotham Books, 2003), 214.
16. Briggs, *Your Child's Self*-Esteem, 201-202.
17. B. J. Bushman, "Does Venting Anger Fee of Extinguish the Flame?" *Personality and Social Psychology Bulletin,*28, 2002, 724-731.
18. Debbie Strong, "7 Ways Anger Is Ruining Your Health," *https://www.everydayhealth.com*, May 29,2015.
19. Briggs, *Your Child's Self*-Esteem, 203.
20. Ibid., 206-207.
21. Handbook for Families, "Dealing with Anger and Contention," *Ensign*, Sept. 1988, 63.
22. *Gospel Doctrine*, 5th ed. (Salt Lake City: Deseret Book, 1939), 316.
23. Neal A. Maxwell, "Behold, the Enemy Is Combined," *Ensign*, May 1993, 79.

24. Ezra Taft Benson, "Fundamentals of Enduring Family Relationships," *Ensign*, Nov. 1982, 60.

Chapter 8
Fostering Confidence

Each chapter of this book has been leading up to and preparing us for the final chapter. As your daily life continues to incorporate proclamation-based principles on a more regular basis, your hoped-for destination will become a reality. The parenting puzzle is nearing completion.

EVALUATION OF USING A PAUSE BUTTON TO CONTROL ANGER AND REFUSING TO ARGUE ASSIGNMENT

Has the use of a pause button been helpful for you in dealing with feelings of anger? Continue to pause before responding in anger and keep refusing to argue. President Gordon B. Hinckley warned of the tragic consequences of anger, asking, "Who can calculate the wounds inflicted, their depth and pain, by harsh and mean words spoken in anger?"[1]

If you have an anger problem, you must acknowledge it and take responsibility for it before you can overcome it. Children may provoke you, but you are responsible for how you respond. Pray with real intent for help in overcoming angry feelings. You can learn to control your anger and respond in better ways.

FOSTERING CONFIDENCE IN CHILDREN

What is the unique destination you envision for your family? Whatever that destination looks like, it will most likely embrace the hope that your children will grow to be confident and resilient individuals. Confident children do better in life. They are healthier, more optimistic, more socially comfortable, and more emotionally secure. When children lack confidence, they are anxious, self-conscious, socially inhibited, frustrated, fearful, and prone to failure. Resilience is being able to bounce back from stress, challenge, tragedy, trauma, or adversity.[2] When children are resilient, they are braver, more curious, more adaptable, and more able to extend their reach into the world. Fostering confidence in our children is a worthy destination.

DEFINITION OF TERMS. Any discussion of fostering confidence must include the importance of building self-esteem. Often the terms self-esteem, self-concept, and self-worth are considered synonymous—but they are not.

Self-worth. Self-worth is a gift from God—infinite and unchanging. We cannot get more self-worth. The jobs we have, the cars we drive, or the clothes we wear do not affect our self-worth—positively or negatively. Our worth is unaffected by the ups and downs of life.

Self-esteem. Our self-esteem is how we *feel* about who we are. It fluctuates for various reasons. A high self-esteem is not conceit but a quiet sense of self-respect. When you have a high self-esteem, you are glad to be you and don't waste time impressing others because you know that you have value.

Self-concept. Our self-concept is what we *believe* ourselves to be and is developed by the age of twelve. Fortunately, our self-concept can be changed. We can't change the past, but we can deal with the present and look to the future.

The importance of positive self-esteem in a child's life cannot be overemphasized. How confident are your children? What can you do to foster greater confidence in them?

PARENTS' RESPONSIBILITY. A parent's first responsibility in nurturing self-esteem in children is to look in the mirror. How do you feel about that person? If you don't like yourself, keep in mind that this attitude is *learned*. Remember: low self-esteem is not a commentary on your value but rather a reflection of the judgments and experiences you have had. *You hold the power of choice* to do something about your low self-esteem. Your own self-image plays a significant role in the quality of the example you set for your children. Take steps to improve your own self-attitudes if needed.

The next responsibility parents have is to meet the two basic needs of children for high self-esteem:

Every child needs to feel lovable. "I matter and have value because I exist."

Every child needs to feel worthwhile and capable. "I can handle myself and my environment with confidence. I know I have something to offer others."

At this point you might be saying, "I *do* love my child and think he is worthwhile." Remember: there is a big difference between *being* loved and *feeling* loved.[3]

WHERE DOES SELF-ESTEEM COME FROM?

Studies show that self-esteem comes from the quality of the relationships that exist between a child and those who are significant to him.[4] We could say that self-esteem comes as we establish a "Come Unto Me" relationship with our children.

♥ Understand child development
♥ Listen to understand
♥ Be kind
♥ Show empathy

Consider the following principles as you strive to help your children gain confidence.

TREAT CHILDREN WITH LOVE AND RESPECT. Children view themselves through the way they are treated by others, especially parents and siblings. When they are loved and accepted, they tend to feel lovable and acceptable. We treat children with love and respect through the effective expression of unconditional love.

Positive eye contact and physical contact send powerful wordless messages, strengthened by our positive words, attitudes, and body language. When we give focused attention and listen to understand feelings, the child thinks, "Dad and Mom like to be with me. They think I'm OK." Children will value themselves to the degree they have been valued.

HELP CHILDREN GAIN FAITH IN GOD. Without faith, no one can have confidence. Children gain great confidence when they feel secure in their relationship with Heavenly Father and their ability to receive spiritual blessings, promises, and direction for their lives. Be deliberate in making spiritual activities a part of everyday life.

HELP CHILDREN DEVELOP PERSONAL INTEGRITY. Parents are the master teachers of values to their children. If parents are honest with their children, children learn honesty. If parents listen and care about their children, children learn to listen and care. Talking is important, but we teach children what we already are. Children learn to value what we actually value—not what we tell them to value or what we say we value—but what we actually value. We must live the values that we say we believe in.

HELP CHILDREN DEVELOP COMPETENCE. Children must learn to work, study, achieve goals, live within rules, and get along with others. As they become competent in those areas, their confidence grows. Research suggests that an organized, clean, and structured home is an optimal setting for the development of resilience. Give children responsibilities and teach them to work by working alongside them, especially when they are young. Be pleasant and patient and try to make work enjoyable for them. Establishing rules and consistent expectations from an early age promotes the development of confidence in young children.

Recognize your children's accomplishments by praising them for their effort regardless of the outcome. In the words of Ezra Taft Benson, "Praise your children more than you correct them. Praise them for even their smallest achievement."[5]

INVOLVE CHILDREN IN SERVING OTHERS. Service projects teach unselfishness and help children to consider the welfare of others. We become more confident individuals as we serve others.

COMPLETING THE PARADIGM SHIFT

In chapter one we noted that a paradigm shift is a distinctly new way of thinking about old problems. The power of experiencing this shift is both exhilarating and humbling. Exhilarating not only because of the new knowledge gained, but because of a whole new way of knowing. Humbling because this knowledge brings a realization that improvements and changes need to be made.

Change is hard. Have you made any changes? Has your paradigm shifted? Parenting is more about changing yourself than changing your children. At this point, the desired outcome is that paradigms have shifted, that hearts have been changed. Listen to the experience one family had with the principle of change.

Stacy and Bill had been in a struggling relationship with their fifteen-year-old daughter for years. In an effort to "save their daughter," they began to study and apply the principles introduced in this book. A few months later Stacy remarked to her daughter, "I feel like our relationship is so much better than it used to be." Her daughter replied, "That's because you and Dad changed."

Stacy was shocked! Sure, she and Bill had tried to be better, but "changed" had never crossed her mind. "It just goes to show," reflected Stacy, "that when we pray for charity, the Lord really does help us—gives us charity, changes our hearts."[6]

WHAT WE HAVE LEARNED. Everything we have discussed throughout the chapters of this book has been for the purpose of raising confident, capable, and resilient children. In addition to the principles already mentioned in this chapter, here is a quick snapshot of some additional truths we have learned:

- ♥ The wisdom of the Parenting Pyramid.
- ♥ The foundation of unconditional love.
- ♥ The power of empathy.
- ♥ The dilemma of a natural parent.

A list of the twelve parenting principles and practices, which were introduced in each chapter, is also included at the end of this chapter. Always remember that principles are like lighthouses because they will light our way. Focusing on principles will have a far greater effect on behavior than focusing on behavior alone.

ONE FINAL STORY. Stories have a way of driving the point home. This final story does just that as it illustrates beautifully what can happen in a home when a parent is able to follow correct principles.

A young father came home from work one day and was met at the door by his three-and-a-half-year-old son, Brenton. Brenton was beaming and said,

Dad, I am a hardworking man!

"Wow," thought Dad. "I wonder why he's feeling so good." After mentioning this interaction to his wife, he found out Brenton's story. Earlier in the day while Mom was downstairs, Brenton had emptied a one-and-a-half-gallon jug of water from the fridge, most of it on the floor. Mom's initial reaction had been to yell at him and spank him. But instead she stopped herself and spoke patiently.

Mom: Brenton, what were you trying to do?

Brenton: I was trying to be a helping man, Mom.

Mom: What do you mean?

Brenton: I washed the dishes for you.

Sure enough, there on the kitchen table were all the dishes he had washed with the water from the water jug.

Mom: Well, honey, why did you use the water from the fridge?

Brenton: I couldn't reach the water in the sink.

Mom: Oh! (looking around) Well, what do you think you could do next time that would make less of a mess?

Brenton thought about it for a minute. Then his face lit up.

Brenton: I could do it in the bathroom!

Mom: The dishes might break in the bathroom. But how about this? What if you came and got me and I helped you move a chair in front of the kitchen sink so that you could do the work there?

Brenton: Good idea!

Mom: Now what shall we do with this mess?

Brenton: Well, we could use a lot of paper towels!

So, Mom gave Brenton some paper towels, and she went and got the mop.

As she was relating this incident to her husband, he realized how important it was that his wife had been able to catch herself between stimulus and response. The important thing here is not having a clean floor. It's raising this boy.

It took her about ten minutes to clean up the mess. If she had reacted to her first inclinations, it also would have taken her about ten minutes, but the difference would have been that Brenton would have met Dad at the door and said,

Daddy, I am a bad boy!

Just think about the difference it made in this family for this mom to consciously act instead of reacting as a natural parent! Brenton could have come out of this experience feeling guilty, embarrassed, and ashamed. But instead he felt affirmed, appreciated, and loved. His good intentions and his desire to help were nurtured. He learned how to help in better ways. His whole attitude about himself and about helping in his home were positively affected by this interaction.[7]

How was Mom able to turn what could have been a very frustrating experience into one that completely filled Brenton's emotional tank? She had a purpose that was bigger than her problem—raising Brenton vs. having a clean floor. In that instant between what happened and her response to it, she was able to connect to that purpose by doing some critical things. She 1) pushed her pause button; 2) realized that children have a reason for doing the things they do; 3) listened to understand that reason; 4) spoke in a kind manner; 5) showed empathy for Brenton.

MEASURING PARENTING SUCCESS

As parents, we often look for indicators of how well we are doing. Do we measure our success as a parent by how well our children turn out—their behaviors, their successes, their failures? Consider this direction given by President Howard W. Hunter:

> A successful parent is one who has loved, one who has sacrificed, and one who has cared for, taught, and ministered to the needs of a child. If you have done all of these and your child is still wayward or troublesome or worldly, it could well be that you are, nevertheless, a successful parent. Perhaps there are children who have come into the world that would challenge any set of parents under any set of circumstances. Likewise, perhaps there are others who would bless the lives of, and be a joy to, almost any father or mother.[8]

REBUILDING A RELATIONSHIP. We all have parenting moments we regret—times when the daunting duties of parenthood overcome us in a way that relationships with our children feel broken or damaged. Or perhaps the child has willfully rebelled, which contributed to the damage. How do we repair such relationships?

To rebuild a relationship with a child, simply increase your demonstration of love for that child through more listening, kindness, patience, understanding, and shared activities. Simultaneously, increase discipline with the child through clear teaching of correct principles and holding the child responsible to meet family expectations and standards. The strength of the parent-child relationship is key to a child's ability to navigate the world and make right choices.

A WORK IN PROGRESS. As a parent, you are a work in progress. Keep in mind the miracle of the Chinese bamboo tree. There are no five-second formulas for change. As with the Chinese bamboo tree, you may not see results for years. But do not be discouraged. The fifth year *will* come.

Remember that you will be off track 90 percent of the time, but that's OK. As long as you know what the track looks like and keep coming back to it time after time, you will succeed.

FINAL ASSIGNMENT

Your final assignment will last for the rest of your life. In addition to the continued practice of all previous assignments, I invite you to pray daily for the gift of charity. This is the most vital habit you will ever establish in your life.

COMPLETING THE PUZZLE

At last we have completed the parenting puzzle. The pieces of a puzzle when standing alone have little value. But as we connect the puzzle piece by piece, a beautiful thing happens. We recognize that these principles aren't new. They have been around for a long time and were taught by Jesus Christ. He taught us how we should care for each other with kindness, persuasion, gentleness, and forgiveness.

Families are the greatest source of happiness in life, and that's what we're all really looking for, isn't it? The most important work we'll ever do will be right in our own homes. There may be challenges to deal with and problems to solve, but in spite of all that—there **are** principles to guide us.

President Gordon B. Hinckley summarizes well our sacred role as parents:

> Never forget that these little ones are the sons and daughters of God and that yours is a custodial relationship to them, that He was a parent before you were parents and that He has not relinquished His parental rights or interest in these His little ones. Now, love them, take care of them. Fathers, control your tempers, now and in all the years to come. Mothers, control your voices, keep them down. Rear your children in love, in the nurture and admonition of the Lord. Take care of your little ones, welcome them into your homes, and nurture and love them with all of your hearts. They may do, in the years that come, some things you would not want them to do, but be patient, be patient. You have not failed as long as you have tried. Never forget that.[9]

For the Rest of Your Life

PRAY FOR THE
GIFT OF CHARITY

STAY ON THE PATH

The closer we follow our Father in Heaven's example and apply His parenting principles, the greater success we will have as parents.

Notes

1. Gordon B. Hinckley, "Our Solemn Responsibilities," *Ensign*, Nov. 1991, 50.
2. Lyle J. Burrup, "Raising Resilient Children," *Ensign*, Mar. 2013, 13.
3. Briggs, *You Child's Self-Esteem*, 3-4.
4. Ibid., 5.
5. Benson, "The Honored Place of Woman," 107.
6. Personal correspondence, used with permission.
7. Covey, *The 7 Habits of Highly Effective Families*, 70-71.
8. Howard W. Hunter, "Parents' Concern for Children," *Ensign*, Nov. 1983. 65.
9. Gordon B. Hinckley, "Excerpts from Recent Addresses of President Gordon B. Hinckley," *Ensign*, July 1997, 73.

Parenting Principles

1. Charity is essential.
2. A child's emotional tank must be filled.
3. You will never be a better parent than you are a person.
4. The quality of the parent/child bond depends upon the quality of the marital bond.
5. All behavioral problems are relationship problems.
6. Feelings must be validated.
7. Order is necessary.
8. Relationships come before rules; unconditional love comes before discipline.
9. Through punishment a parent controls a child's actions; through good discipline a parent teaches a child to control his own actions.
10. Work is a blessing and not only promotes happiness but teaches responsibility.
11. Misbehavior in children must not be condoned.
12. Anger is the destroyer of family relations.

Parenting Practices

1. Pray daily for the gift of charity.
2. Fill a child's emotional tank by expressing unconditional love to the child.
3. Practice the "Magic Five to Stay Alive."
4. Nurture the marriage relationship.
5. Build a "Come Unto Me" relationship.
6. Practice Emotion Coaching in parent/child relationships.
7. Establish and enforce family rules.
8. Build and maintain a "Come Unto Me" relationship with children.
9. Use discipline rather than punishment with children.
10. Organize children's work.
11. Use the authoritative parenting style.
12. Be an example to children by using an appropriate coping strategy to control anger.

THE FAMILY

A PROCLAMATION TO THE WORLD

THE FIRST PRESIDENCY AND COUNCIL OF THE TWELVE APOSTLES OF THE CHURCH OF JESUS CHRIST OF LATTER-DAY SAINTS

WE, THE FIRST PRESIDENCY and the Council of the Twelve Apostles of The Church of Jesus Christ of Latter-day Saints, solemnly proclaim that marriage between a man and a woman is ordained of God and that the family is central to the Creator's plan for the eternal destiny of His children.

ALL HUMAN BEINGS—male and female—are created in the image of God. Each is a beloved spirit son or daughter of heavenly parents, and, as such, each has a divine nature and destiny. Gender is an essential characteristic of individual premortal, mortal, and eternal identity and purpose.

IN THE PREMORTAL REALM, spirit sons and daughters knew and worshipped God as their Eternal Father and accepted His plan by which His children could obtain a physical body and gain earthly experience to progress toward perfection and ultimately realize their divine destiny as heirs of eternal life. The divine plan of happiness enables family relationships to be perpetuated beyond the grave. Sacred ordinances and covenants available in holy temples make it possible for individuals to return to the presence of God and for families to be united eternally.

THE FIRST COMMANDMENT that God gave to Adam and Eve pertained to their potential for parenthood as husband and wife. We declare that God's commandment for His children to multiply and replenish the earth remains in force. We further declare that God has commanded that the sacred powers of procreation are to be employed only between man and woman, lawfully wedded as husband and wife.

WE DECLARE the means by which mortal life is created to be divinely appointed. We affirm the sanctity of life and of its importance in God's eternal plan.

HUSBAND AND WIFE have a solemn responsibility to love and care for each other and for their children. "Children are an heritage of the Lord" (Psalm 127:3). Parents have a sacred duty to rear their children in love and righteousness, to provide for their physical and spiritual needs, and to teach them to love and serve one another, observe the commandments of God, and be law-abiding citizens wherever they live. Husbands and wives—mothers and fathers—will be held accountable before God for the discharge of these obligations.

THE FAMILY is ordained of God. Marriage between man and woman is essential to His eternal plan. Children are entitled to birth within the bonds of matrimony, and to be reared by a father and a mother who honor marital vows with complete fidelity. Happiness in family life is most likely to be achieved when founded upon the teachings of the Lord Jesus Christ. Successful marriages and families are established and maintained on principles of faith, prayer, repentance, forgiveness, respect, love, compassion, work, and wholesome recreational activities. By divine design, fathers are to preside over their families in love and righteousness and are responsible to provide the necessities of life and protection for their families. Mothers are primarily responsible for the nurture of their children. In these sacred responsibilities, fathers and mothers are obligated to help one another as equal partners. Disability, death, or other circumstances may necessitate individual adaptation. Extended families should lend support when needed.

WE WARN that individuals who violate covenants of chastity, who abuse spouse or offspring, or who fail to fulfill family responsibilities will one day stand accountable before God. Further, we warn that the disintegration of the family will bring upon individuals, communities, and nations the calamities foretold by ancient and modern prophets.

WE CALL UPON responsible citizens and officers of government everywhere to promote those measures designed to maintain and strengthen the family as the fundamental unit of society.

This proclamation was read by President Gordon B. Hinckley as part of his message at the General Relief Society Meeting held September 23, 1995, in Salt Lake City, Utah.

About the Author

Marsha Snow, an Arizona native, received her BGS degree with an emphasis in family life from Brigham Young University. She has studied, researched, and taught classes about parenting for many years. Marsha and her husband, Paul, are the parents of six children and the grandparents of twenty-four.

Made in the USA
Las Vegas, NV
07 December 2020

12253997R00085